Internationalism in Practice

CLAUDIA JONES,
BLACK LIBERATION,
AND THE "BESTIAL" WAR ON KOREA

Internationalism in Practice

CLAUDIA JONES,
BLACK LIBERATION,
AND THE "BESTIAL" WAR ON KOREA

Claudia Jones

FEATURING CONTRIBUTIONS FROM

BETSY YOON
DENISE LYNN
GERALD HORNE
TIONNE PARRIS
KIM IL SUNG

Published by *Iskra Books* 2024

All rights reserved.
The moral rights of the author have been asserted.

Jones' articles in the present volume are reproduced kindly and with gratitude from the theoretical journal, *Political Affairs* (1949, 1950, 1952), of the CPUSA.

Iskra Books
www.iskrabooks.org
US | UK | Ireland

Iskra Books is an independent scholarly publisher—publishing original works of revolutionary theory, history, education, and art, as well as edited collections, new translations, and critical republications of older works.

ISBN-13: 979-8-8691-3160-7 (Softcover)

British Library Cataloguing in Publication Data
A catalogue record for this book is available from the British Library.

Library of Congress Cataloging-in-Publication Data
A catalog record for this book is available from the Library of Congress

Cover Art by Ben Stahnke
Editing, Proofing, and Typesetting by David Peat

CONTENTS

EDITOR'S NOTE   vii

SECTION 1: INTRODUCTIONS

70 Years of Black and Korean Internationalism
Publisher's Introduction   1

Essay on the 70th Anniversary of the Fatherland Liberation War Victory
Betsy Yoon   8

SECTION 2: THEORETICAL FOUNDATIONS

The Theory of Super-Exploitation
Denise Lynn   15

An End to the Neglect of the Problems of the Negro Woman!
Claudia Jones   21

SECTION 3: ANTI-IMPERIALISM AT THE HEIGHT OF THE ANTI-COMMUNIST WITCH HUNT

International Women's Day as a New Day against Imperialism
Liberation School   41

International Women's Day and the Struggle for Peace
Claudia Jones   46

For the Unity of Women in the Cause of Peace!
Claudia Jones   62

The Struggle for Peace in the United States
Claudia Jones   83

Statement Before Being Sentenced to One Year and a Day Imprisonment
Claudia Jones   106

Section 4: Conclusions

"Negro Women Can Think and Speak and Write!" Jones' Speech to the Court Before Her Sentencing
Gerald Horne & Tionne Parris   115

The Great Anti-Imperialist Revolutionary Cause of Asian, African, and Latin American Peoples is Invincible
Kim Il Sung   119

Contributors   132

Farewell to Claudia
Elizabeth Gurley Flynn   133

Editor's Note

Historical articles have been edited slightly for clarity. Additional contextual information is provided by footnotes beginning with [**Ed. Note:**]. All other footnotes have been preserved from the originals.

SECTION 1
Introductions

70 Years of Black and Korean Internationalism:
An Opportunity and Responsibility for the U.S. Left Today

Publisher's Introduction

Throughout the years of the global struggle between the oppressors and the oppressed, 1953 was especially significant, situated as it was in a complex and highly dynamic and unpredictable conjuncture. A wide variety of elements across the world condensed into decisive turning points that solidified beyond all doubt the contradictory development of the global revolutionary offensive and its counterrevolutionary defensive. As far as years are useful for marking history, especially in regular discussions, 1953 is one that, in many ways, continues to define the revolutionary struggle of today. That was the year Stalin died, the Korean resistance forced the U.S. to sign an Armistice Agreement, and the year Claudia Jones was, along with other leaders of the Communist Party, found guilty of violating the Smith Act and sentenced to over a year in prison. A year of defeats and victories, these three seemingly disconnected events were intimately bound together, as the original essays and Jones' original articles assembled in what follows make abundantly clear.

When much of the world awoke to the news on March 6, 1953, they learned that the night before, shortly before 10:00 pm, Joseph V. Stalin, who guided the Soviet Union for decades, had passed away. The world's official leaders awaited with anticipation and anxiety for what was to come. Given Stalin's prestige across the world and how many dissolved his personality into the Soviet Union and the communist movement (rather than the other way around), would Stalin's death dissolve that movement? Would internecine battles within the Communist Party of the Soviet Union's leadership empower reactionary forces or at least open cracks for imperialist intervention? As it turns out, both happened in some form, as the U.S. seized on the intra-party struggles to further drive a wedge between the increasingly uncomradely debates between the Soviet and Chinese communists.

Those from the progressive countries worried about the fate of their primary ally and source of aid and solidarity for these reasons and others. Most progressive forces worldwide were, of course, in mourning. This includes those living in the heartland of world imperialism, the U.S. Perhaps the most significant was Black revolutionary William Edward Burghardt Du Bois. A long-time supporter of the communist struggle, Du Bois wrote not one but two eulogies for the historic figure. "Joseph Stalin was a great man; few other men of the 20th century approach his stature," opened one short statement. Published under the title, "Dr. Du Bois on Stalin: 'He knew the common man [...] followed his fate,'" it appeared in the March 16, 1953 edition of the independent left-wing newspaper the *National Guardian* based out of New York City." As one of the despised minorities of man," Du Bois continued, "he first set Russia on the road to conquer race prejudice and make one nation out of its 140 groups without destroying their individuality," continued Du Bois with a U.S. readership in mind.[1] Whereas Du Bois noted the Soviet Union's emphasis on eliminating racial and national oppression in his first eulogy, the second highlighted the international response and appreciation of that concrete solidarity. "The death of Joseph Stalin," he begins, "shocked 15 million American citizens of Negro descent in a peculiar way. Stalin had unequivocally advocated Peace while all other rulers voiced two words for War to every one for Peace. These Negroes want peace for more reasons than whites."[2] As contemporary revolutionary communist scholars have noted, this wasn't the first time Du Bois went to bat for his friends in the Communist Party or the Soviet Union, and it wouldn't be the last.[3]

---

1   W.E.B. Du Bois, "On Stalin," *National Guardian* 5, no. 16 (1953): p. 4.

2   W.E.B. Du Bois, "Stalin and American Negroes," *Pravda*, 10 March 1953. Reprinted in *Peace, Land, and Bread* 05 March 2021. Available here: www.peacelandbread.org/post/w-e-b-du-bois-s-stalin-and-american-negroes.

3   See Derek R. Ford, *Communist Study: Education for the Commons*, 2nd ed.

In 1950, an issue of the *Negro Digest* featured a symposium on a remark Paul Robeson made the year before about Black people and their inherent comradery with the Soviet Union. The *Negro Digest* was the personal project of Black businessman John Harold Johnson, who collected funding for the first installments with personal appeals for pre-paid subscriptions before, eventually, partnering with Joseph Levy, a magazine publisher. After hitting Chicago newsstands in late 1942, the *Negro Digest* became one of many Black periodicals of the period, although it distinguished itself by including a range of voices across the political spectrum and the overall editorial line established by Johnson: a patriotic belief that the U.S. could be a real democracy.[4] The *Digest* featured a regular column on the back page, "If I Were a Negro," to which Eleanor Roosevelt contributed in the magazine's February 1943 edition. This provides a sense not only of the magazine's political orientation and its process of popularization and funding, but also the context in which the symposium appeared.

Du Bois defended Robeson in the Symposium, which focused specifically a comment made in Paris on April 20, 1949. As he entered the room, the audience erupted in thunderous cheers, which quieted after approaching the stage. There, Du Bois recalls, "his great voice rose in song—song of Black slaves, song of white slaves, songs of Russia and France," followed by a short speech in which he stated, "the black folk of America will never fight against the Soviet Union!" again to great applause.[5] Robeson was right; he knew what he was talking about. He wasn't afraid to speak the truth even though he knew it would—and did—stir immense controversy in the U.S., within the political elite, the Black bourgeoisie, and factions of the Black press. Robeson's knowledge, Du Bois insists, wasn't abstract. His knowledge came from the time he had spent in the USSR and the U.S. "He knew better than most men," Du Bois continues, "that of all countries, Russia alone has made race prejudice a crime; of all great imperialisms Russia alone owns no colonies of dark serfs or white and what is more important has no investments in colonies and is lifting no blood-soaked profits from cheap

---

(Lanham: Lexington Books, 2022); and "Against the 'Compatible' Academic Left: Rethinking Capitalism and Racism," *PESA Agora*, 2023. Available here: https://pesaagora.com/columns/against-the-compatible-radical-academic-left.

4   Nichols Grant, "*The Negro Digest*: Race, Exceptionalism and the Second World War," *Journal of American Studies* 52, no. 2 (2018): pp. 358-389.

5   William Edward Burghardt Du Bois, "Symposium: Paul Robeson: Right or Wrong?" *Negro Digest* 7, no. 8 (1950): p.5.

labor in Asia and Africa."⁶ Indeed, immediately after taking power, the Bolsheviks unconditionally renounced their "rights" to foreign territories and exposed the secret imperialist agreements about what country would get what colony.

The figure most thoroughly demonized and caricatured in the West, Joseph Stalin, earned the respect of many Black U.S. and African revolutionaries. This is why it is noteworthy that Du Bois, for example, joined the Communist Party *after* Nikita Khrushchev's 1956 'Secret Speech' that established a right-wing critique of Stalin and irreparably damaged the international communist movement because from then on, as Domenico Losurdo writes "it was only Stalin and his closest collaborators who were confined to the museum of horrors" and the cause of every problem faced by the Soviet Union or the imperialist U.S.⁷ The Soviets, understandably eager to avoid another World War, pursued a nuclear non-proliferation treaty with the U.S., something that was intolerable to the People's Republic of China for equally understandable reasons.

It was not that anyone *wanted* war or nuclear war, but that the USSR-US pact was, in effect, an anti-China pact. The issue of peace was on the forefront of the international progressive agenda in 1953 as U.S. war against Korea reignited a long-standing Black desire for peace. Du Bois enunciates the basis of unity between Black Americans and Koreans in one of his obituaries. "Koreans were Colored People," he writes, who had "suffered from white nations, the same discrimination and contempt as Negroes suffer."⁸

Du Bois, like Robeson, knew how the Third International worked to help the oppressed free themselves and the real material gains that resulted. They were aware, too, of the contradictions that entailed, the errors made, and the formulaic applications of abstract principles to different contexts. Nonetheless, from Cuba and Guyana to Zimbabwe and Syria—not to mention China—there was an ideological and affective bond linking them together. That bond is the Global Class Struggle that continues to this day.

---

6   Ibid., p. 10.

7   Domenico Losurdo, *Stalin: History and Critique of a Black Legend*, trans. H. Hakamäki and Salvatore Engel-Di Mauro (Madison: Iskra Books, 2023), p. 9.

8   Du Bois, "Stalin and American Negroes," *Pravda*, 1953.

Revolutionary Black Internationalism and Korean Solidarity

Claudia Jones echoed Du Bois and Robeson's shared understanding of the Korean and U.S. Black liberation struggles. Shared, of course, does not mean uniform, and one of Jones' great contributions was her ability to identify the unique position of Black women workers in the U.S. in the struggle against imperialist wars. She recognized her fellow Black women workers as being those who would first spontaneously recognize the internationalist position of Black people in the U.S. and their Korean comrades, who were united in part by a common enemy: U.S. imperialism largely. This system was, after all, built on the super-exploitation of enslaved Africans, Black workers of all genders, and the colonial and imperialist plunder of the world.

In the coming pages, we will see Claudia Jones emphasize this point repeatedly, although she will add the unique position of Black women in resisting imperialist wars and in being among the first to recognize the shared position of Black people in the U.S. and their Korean comrades. One prominent instance Jones did so was about a month before Du Bois' wrote the above passages and in quite dire circumstances. Having been convicted of several charges, among them conspiring to overthrow the U.S. government, with 13 other communist leaders in January, Jones delivered a statement in front of Judge Edward J. Dimrock before receiving her sentencing on February 2, 1953. Jones wasn't speaking to the judge or the U.S. state, both of which she viewed as impotent, but to the real force in the world: the global peace movement. Jones begins articulating her hope that her statement might "even one whit to further dedicate growing millions of Americans to fight for peace and to repel the fascist drive on free speech and thought in our country."[9]

In her speech reprinted here and brilliantly contextualized and expounded upon by Gerald Horne and Tionne Parris, Jones mentions how the prosecution used her 1950 International Women's Day speech, published in *Political Affairs*, as evidence against her. However, though it was introduced, it wasn't read aloud. Jones asserted this was because "it urges American mothers, Negro women and white, to emulate the peace struggles of their anti-fascist sisters in Latin America, in the new European democracies, in the Soviet Union, in Asia and Africa to end the bestial Korean war [...] to reject the militarist threat to embroil us in a war with China, so that their children should not suffer the fate of the Korean babies murdered by napalm bombs of B-29s, or the fate of Hi-

---

9   Jones, *Statement Before Being Sentenced...* [see this volume, p. 106].

roshima."[10] The Korean people almost suffered from nuclear weapons and most of the Pentagon and U.S. foreign policy establishment were anxious to deploy them not only against Pyongyang but Beijing as well. Yet there is no reason or basis on which to compare the destruction of U.S. imperialism across the world.

A few months after Stalin's death and Jones' speech, the Korean people, led by the Korean People's Army and in collaboration with their Chinese comrades, forced the U.S. to sign an armistice agreement that finally halted their "police action." What the U.S. calls the Korean War and the north Koreans and progressives refer to as the Great Fatherland Liberation War came to an end as "the heroic struggle waged by the Korean people for three years in defense of the country's freedom and independence against the U.S. imperialist armed invaders ended in victory for us" and defeat for the imperialists.[11] The war looked to many like a conflict between two different states, each claiming sovereignty over the other's territory. This framing avoids the essence of the struggle and distorts the global nature of the U.S.'s military aggression.

Kim Il Sung, the primary leader of the decades-long anti-colonial struggle and later of the struggle to force U.S. imperialists out of the northern half of Korea, endorsed this internationalist position. For example, Kim begins his "1946 Report to the Second Congress of the Workers' Party of North Korea" with an assessment of the post-World War II international climate and defined them relative to the radically altered position of two camps. "The most essential of these changes," Kim begins, "is that the capitalist system, that is, the reactionary Imperialist camp, has become markedly weaker, whereas the international democratic camp headed by the Soviet Union has come into being and has definitely gained in strength."[12] Among the latter camp, Kim includes "the great force of the oppressed peoples who have risen in the struggle to achieve national freedom and independence against colonialism."[13]

---

10   Ibid. [see this volume p. 109].

11   Kim Il Sung, "Everything for the Postwar Rehabilitation and Development of the National Economy," in *Kim Il Sung Selected Works (Vol. 1)* (Pyongyang: Foreign Languages Publishing House, 1953/1976), p. 415.

12   Kim Il Sung, "Report to the Second Congress of the Workers' Party of North Korea," in *Kim Il Sung Selected Works (Vol. 1)* (Pyongyang: Foreign Languages Publishing House, 1955/1976), pp. 204-205.

13   Ibid., p. 213.

A Relation of Reciprocity: A Legacy of Inspiration

While Du Bois paid tributes and expressed his sorrow to the people of the world in his obituaries of Stalin, Kim Il Sung wrote to Du Bois' widow, Shirley Graham Du Bois, after learning of his death in 1963. "On receiving the sad news of Dr. William Du Bois' Death," Kim wrote before clarifying the late Du Bois' credentials as a "distinguished peace champion and scholar," President Kim—or as the Premier of the Cabinet of the DPRK as he was known at the time—sent his "profound condolences" to her and the family on behalf of the DPRK. He assured her that Du Bois' "unflinching struggle against the racial discrimination policy and for the safeguarding of peace" would not be forgotten by the Korean people. In the letter dated September 2, Kim concluded by reminding her that her late husband and comrade's contributions would only strengthen the resolve of oppressed peoples until our collective "final victory."[14] So too should the writings that follow and the outcomes of their authors and theorists embolden our commitments to establish a revolutionary wing in the rising social movements of the U.S. in a careful and strategic manner and to wave unflinchingly, as Jones and Kim did, against all manifestations of national chauvinism, sexism, white supremacy, and imperialism.

We are confident that—given Iskra's growing reputation and audience, the tremendous scholars commenting on Jones' works, and the increasingly revolutionary, anti-racist, and anti-imperialist forces leading the movements in the U.S. today—this book will do for contemporary struggles what it did for President Kim and the Korean struggle. That will not happen on its own, of course. So let this book not only be read but *acted upon* in daily interactions as well as large-scale actions. The authors and editors who have worked to assemble this superb, accessible publication have done the international struggle for justice and liberation an immense favor. We must, in every opportunity, seek to advance the class struggle, which is inseparable today from the national liberation struggles inside and outside of the U.S. prison house of nations.

---

14   Kim Il Sung, "Accra Madame Shirley Graham Du Bois," 02 September 1963, *W.E.B. Du Bois Papers* (MS 312) Special Collections and University Archives (University of Massachusetts, Amherst Libraries), pp. 2-3.

Essay on the 70ᵗʰ Anniversary of the Fatherland Liberation War Victory

Betsy Yoon

A lot has been written about Korea, the Korean War, and the armistice. Yet an understanding of the armistice, the unresolved nature of the war, and the implications for today remain absent from most mainstream narratives about Korea. When either north or south Korea appear in the headlines, the historical conditions that lay at the root of today's circumstances—and particularly the United States' role in creating those conditions—are rarely mentioned. In fact, the Korean War itself is also known as "the Forgotten War." But what does forgetting mean when the forgetting refers to an ongoing situation rather than a past event?

The appellation of the Forgotten War is not accidental; what is highlighted and commemorated on a national level in the United States serves to sustain imperialist interests. This pattern is not unique to Korea and manifests in discourses about many ongoing sites of liberation struggle. In Palestine, for example, through this lens of selective forgetting and remembering, occupation is framed as "conflict" and acts of resistance are framed as terrorism.

In terms of the Korean peninsula, the U.S. would like for it to be forgotten that Korea has been unified for longer than it has been divided.

The U.S. would like for it to be forgotten that the war remains unresolved. The U.S. would like for the realities of U.S. war in Korea to be forgotten: massacres, carpet bombing, and the threat of nuclear war. And the U.S. would like for us to think that the U.S. is an agent of peace and humanity on the Korean peninsula. We are not to remember that south Korea does not even have the sovereign right of operational control over its military should active war break out, or that north Korea is burdened with debilitating sanctions that disproportionately affect the most vulnerable.

Liberal narratives around past struggles commonly invoke the refrain of, "Oh, if only we had known." For example, with Iraq's nonexistent WMDs, if only we had known they didn't actually have WMDs. The implication is that a lack of information is at the root of past injustices and that with sufficient information, things like massacres, displacement, and murder through economic blockade would not be permitted to happen. But as we see from the writings of Claudia Jones, there were those who understood and named what the U.S. was doing in Korea as it was happening, and how this related to conditions at home.

In the writings collected in this book, Jones lays out the need to forge and develop links between arenas that are today often thought to be separate. In particular, Jones makes clear that in order to be truly anti-war, one must be anti-imperialist. In her March 1950 speech on International Women's Day, for example, Jones says, "a fundamental condition for rallying the masses of American women into the peace camp is to free them from the influence of the agents of imperialism." In this one speech—given months before the official outbreak of the Korean War—Jones condemned the "bipartisan war policy" of the Truman Administration, called for an end to atomic bomb production, put forth the need for a united front firmly rooted in working class anti-imperialism, and drew clear connections between the fight for peace, U.S. wars, and class struggle. These were not separate topics but deeply connected. Following the example set by Jones, this chapter will provide some historical background and discuss both the past and present-day implications of the armistice.

Historical Background

A dilemma that faces anyone writing or thinking about any national liberation struggle is the question of where to start and what level of granularity is required for an accurate understanding of present-day circumstances. While this text offers some critical historical flashpoints, it is not a history. The points offered here seek to answer the question of, what is most helpful for understanding the context of the armistice? How can we appropriately assess the unresolved Korean War and its continuing impact? These flashpoints or components are framed through an understanding that imperialism was a driving factor in developments on the Korean peninsula from the beginning of the 20th century to the present day. Given this understanding, I begin with the following flashpoint: the Taft-Katsura Memorandum of 1905.

In a desire to maintain a foothold in Asia, and in the face of Japan's military gains against China and Russia in the late 19th century, in 1905 the United States negotiated an agreement with Japan regarding spheres of influence. Known as the Taft-Katsura Memorandum (named after U.S. Secretary of War William Howard Taft and Japanese Prime Minister Katsura Tarō), "the United States recognized Japan's right to control Korea in exchange for Japan's acceptance of U.S. hegemony over the Philippines."[1] Japan turned Korea into a protectorate that same year and formally annexed Korea in 1910, ushering in 35 years of harsh colonial rule.

Taft-Katsura clearly locates the Korean struggle in U.S. imperial expansion, as Claudia Jones does. Thus we see that the struggle in Asia—from the Philippines to China to Korea—is the same struggle against U.S. imperialism. As Lenin noted, one of the features of imperialism is "the territorial division of the whole world among the biggest capitalist powers."[2] This moment demonstrates the common roots of present-day struggles in the Philippines and the Korean peninsula and demonstrates the need for solidarity across Asia against imperialism. We must be engaged in the struggle that is before us: a global struggle against imperialism in which the futures of all nations fighting for national liberation are tied together.

The material conditions of colonization laid the groundwork for conditions in a liberated Korea in 1945. While the Soviet Union was in position to receive Japan's surrender and oversee Japan's exit from Korea, the United States, already thinking of their wartime ally as an enemy and

---

1 Martin Hart-Landsberg, *Korea: Division, Reunification, and U.S. Foreign Policy* (New York, NY: Monthly Review Press, 1998, p. 26).

2 Vladimir Ilyich Lenin, *Imperialism: The Highest Stage of Capitalism* (Paris: Foreign Language Press, 2020).

not wanting the Soviet Union to operate unchallenged in the region, proposed a division of Korea along the 38th parallel, wherein the United States would accept Japan's surrender below this dividing line. Thus we see the direct path from Taft-Katsura to colonization to division to war, leading to the past 70 years of an armistice and an unresolved war.

Armistice

The armistice is synonymous with a continued state of division; when talking about the armistice, it is therefore necessary to also talk about division and reunification. The state of the armistice and the continued state of division is not only a structural feature that represses and limits the full potential and self-determination of the Korean people on both sides of the DMZ, but it also is a key component to sustaining U.S. imperialism in the Asia-Pacific region, and, given the strategic importance of maritime access to shipping lanes in the area, on a global level.

This division has led to divided ways of remembering events on the peninsula. As Kim Dong-Choon points out, in south Korea, the war is often remembered just by the date on which it began, June 25.[3] It's called either the Korean war or 6.25; in contrast, north Korea refers to it as the Fatherland Liberation War. The narrative in south Korea is more aligned with the U.S. narrative that frames the Korean war as a conflict between Koreans that the U.S. intervened in for moral reasons. Understanding the war as a Fatherland Liberation War places the Korean war in its historical context—that of a national liberation from Japan that was interrupted by the United States. This differentiated national remembering of the Korean War manifests around the armistice as well. Located north of the DMZ, the building in which the armistice was signed has been turned into a site of remembering. Visitors are told that the U.S. wanted to sign the armistice in a temporary structure, but north Korea felt that it should be commemorated and preserved and so built a permanent structure for the proceedings. Accordingly, the armistice in north Korea is celebrated as a victory and is a national holiday. In contrast, this event is not celebrated in south Korea (there are organizations in the south that do commemorate the armistice, but it is not a national holiday). And in fact, south Korea was not a signatory to the armistice. The fact that the armistice was implemented without the participation of one of the two Koreas lends credence to the notion that this war was

---

3   Kim Dong-Choon, *The Unending Korean War: A Social History* (CA: Tamal Vista Publications, 2000, p. 3).

not simply a war between Koreans but was in fact a liberation war.

When discussing the armistice, it is also important to remember that the war could have been over by 1951, rather than 1953. The two sides had reached a stalemate by mid-1951, and agreed to begin talks to end the war. "Expectations on the North Korean side were that it would take only a few days to reach an accord. [...] The war continued largely because the U.S. government refused to stop fighting until all outstanding issues [...] had been settled."[4] Again, this was knowable both then and now: Jones was calling for an end to the Korean war in 1951, in full awareness that this was a U.S. war and that the U.S. had the power to end it.[5] Every step of the way, the U.S. has been against peace in Korea, and just as it obstructed efforts to stop active fighting in the Korean war for two years, it has continued to obstruct efforts to formally end the war for 70 years.

The armistice was meant to be one point along a continuum of progress toward peace, never the endpoint. And yet, after 70 years, we find ourselves not only with an armistice still intact but with increasing militarization and tension. Heightened tensions and increased risk of war are not unfortunate side effects of the armistice; they are the only possible outcome.

Impact of the Armistice

Since the armistice, the threat of north Korea has been regularly used as justification for ongoing militarization of the peninsula. Most recently this rationale was invoked when describing the formation of the Nuclear Consultative Group in summer 2023,[6] which was coordinated with the docking of nuclear-capable ballistic missile submarines in Busan and Jeju Island, returning nuclear weapons to south Korea for the first time since 1994, when the U.S. announced the removal of nuclear weapons they had previously covertly stationed in south Korea.

This same rationale was used when installing the Terminal High Al-

---

4　Hart-Landsberg, *Korea*, p. 130.

5　Jones, "For the Unity of Women in the Cause of Peace!" [see this volume, p. 62].

6　Victor Cha, "The U.S.-ROK Nuclear Consultative Group's Successful Launching," *Center for Strategic and International Studies*, July 20, 2023. Available here: https://www.csis.org/analysis/us-rok-nuclear-consultative-groups-successful-launching

titude Area Defense system (THAAD), displacing residents of Seongju and for the construction of the naval base that displaced villagers in Gangjeong on Jeju Island. The United States is aggressively militarizing its forces on the Korean peninsula, with north Korea as the justification. But as we are reminded by Taft-Katsura, the U.S. is not just interested in Korea itself, but in what Korea represents strategically and regionally. North Korea, the armistice, and the unresolved war serve as a convenient cover for the U.S.'s primary desire to contain China and maintain the free flow of capital in the region.

Conclusion

Removing the condition of the armistice is one necessary component to weakening U.S. imperialist designs in East Asia. As with any component, resolving the armistice and the Korean War is only one step, it is not the end goal. A peaceful resolution to the unresolved Korean war, much less the dismantlement of imperialism, will require more than moving from an armistice to some kind of peace agreement. But it is a necessary component.

Let us follow in the footsteps of Claudia Jones, who demonstrates not only that we don't need to wait for the benefit of hindsight but also how imperialism drove seemingly disparate struggles as the Korean liberation struggle and class struggle in the U.S. Hindsight is only useful if we use it to inform how we approach the present. We have had 70 years of hindsight and the path forward is clear. Resolve the armistice and end the Korean War!

SECTION 2
Theoretical Foundations

The Theory of Super-Exploitation

Denise Lynn

Claudia Jones was one of the most prolific and impactful theoreticians in the U.S. left. After joining the Communist Party (CPUSA), her work in its publications led her to engage with and challenge Party policy and practice and its ongoing conversation with Marxist-Leninist theory. Jones produced important work throughout her years in the CPUSA, and her most influential article, "An End to the Neglect of the Problems of the Negro Woman!"—published in 1949—laid the foundation for expanding the Party's analysis on Black women's oppression. More importantly, as other scholars have noted, the article helped to influence Black Left Feminism and movement-building among later generations of activists.

While women's World War II contributions have been celebrated in U.S. culture, their crushed aspirations after the war have largely been ignored. After 1945, women faced job loss, a suppression of political organizing, and the ascendance of a conservative ideology that reified the white heteronormative nuclear family as the "traditional" familial structure and sought to isolate middle class white women within its confines. Black women and working women remained outside that construction and were deeply impacted by the loss of higher-paying war jobs and the short-lived childcare subsidies that enabled war work. This evidenced, for Jones, that women's labor, both productive and reproductive, was valued but expendable in the war state.

Anti-communism's dominance in these years caused membership

problems for the Communist Party but created the possibility for women in its ranks to challenge sex chauvinism and to expand Marxist-Leninist thinking on the "Woman Question." Party women had been theorizing gender oppression within the Marxist-Leninist canon for years, and, as Kate Weigand argues, the Party became more receptive to these articulations after WWII, at a time when it was embattled by anti-communist harassment but committed to movement-building and drawing in new members.

Betty Millard published the pamphlet *Woman Against Myth* in 1948 which has since been credited with challenging the CPUSA to rethink its assumptions that women were an oppressed class. Millard pointed to the social and cultural infrastructures that operated alongside economic disenfranchisement, working to keep women confined to limited roles, and she challenged the traditional Marxist cosmology which assumed that class struggle alone would emancipate women. Millard also exposed sex chauvinism among her fellow leftists and noted that while socialism created the conditions that could usher in liberation, socialists had to actively address sexism and sexist institutions. The pamphlet, however, universalized women's experiences and failed to account for racist oppression; it also neglected to recognize racism within the ranks of the left.[1]

These elisions were one inspiration for Jones to write her "Neglect" article. The other inspiration was the lynch law case of Rosa Lee Ingram. Lynch law was a phrase the Party used to describe the legal lynching of Black defendants in the U.S. criminal legal system.

Ingram was a widowed sharecropper who, along with her sons, killed her white neighbor while trying to fight off his sexual advances. She and her sons were arrested, tried, and sentenced to death. Jones believed that Ingram's case embodied the peril in failing to acknowledge Black women's "super-exploitation" as a worker, woman, and Black American. As a Black sharecropper and a woman in rural Georgia, Ingram struggled to achieve the economic wherewithal to support her family; as a Black woman, she was vulnerable to the lecherous advances of her white neighbor; as a Black American, she would not find justice in the criminal legal system.[2]

---

1 Kate Weigand, *Red Feminism: American Communism and the Making of Women's Liberation* (Baltimore: Johns Hopkins University, 2001), pp. 67-68.

2 Cheryl Higashida, *Black Internationalist Feminism: Women Writers of the Black Left, 1945-1995* (Urbana: University of Illinois Press, 2011), p. 57.

Jones' "Neglect" article focuses on three themes—Black women's historical and contemporary triple oppression, white chauvinism among progressives, and key areas of struggle where Black women's leadership could advance the movement. Jones's analysis pivoted on the argument that the triply oppressed Black woman had been radicalized by U.S. white supremacist capitalism and that the fatal error of progressives was ignoring the historical and contemporary leadership of the Black woman. She believed that to focus on Black women's emancipation meant dismantling the class, race, and gender structures that delimited all the oppressed and, therefore, created the space to liberate everyone. Carole Boyce Davies describes this as the "neglect thesis" which positioned Black women's emancipation as key to the liberation of all the oppressed.

Activists had long recognized Black women's unique oppression, but it was Jones who integrated that analysis into the Marxist canon, thus making her "Left of Karl Marx," as Boyce Davies argues. Jones' colleague Louise Thompson Patterson described "triple exploitation" in a 1936 article on Black domestic laborers. After World War II, Jones would take the analysis further and emphasize Black women's "triple oppression" and argue that it positioned them as uniquely capable of leadership because of their historical militancy and resistance to that oppression.[3]

To prove this assertion, Jones argued that Black women were radical militants with decades of experience in resistance because of several historical conditions: the first was that the enslaved marriage was not recognized, and Black women were often kept from their partners or sexually assaulted and impregnated by white men. Under slave law, children followed the condition of the mother—because of this, the children resulting from sexual assaults or from partnerships with enslaved men were themselves enslaved. After emancipation, Black women faced economic and political disenfranchisement, legal and extralegal lynching, sexual harassment, and assault. These historical conditions meant that they had been at the forefront of racist, sexist, and capitalist resistance to protect the precarious material conditions of the Black family. Jones's article counseled her white comrades to recognize this and to correct their exclusion from Party leadership. Jones exemplified these possibilities; she was radicalized by racist and sexist oppression and embodied

---

3   Carole Boyce Davies, *Left of Karl Marx: The Political Life of Black Communist Claudia Jones* (Durham: Duke University Press, 2007), pp. 38-39.

the leadership capabilities the Party needed.

Millard's analysis recognized that sexism infected the United States and that even in the socialist USSR, sexist traditions were slow to disappear—but socialism also enabled women to achieve liberation. Jones's issue with Millard's pamphlet was that it elided racist struggles and demonstrated what Party members called "race chauvinism."

Jones took Party members to task for their failure to recognize and correct their own prejudices. She described paternalistic Party members who dismissed Black women members and who engaged in racist practices including condescension about domestic laborers, holding to bourgeois beauty standards that valued light-skin, rejecting interracial relationships, and continuing to educate their children in segregated institutions.

The treatment of domestic labor, a field dominated by Black women, exemplified progressives' white chauvinism. Jones argued that not only was domestic labor ignored under federal and state protections, but labor unions failed to recognize it, and that some Party members in fact sought out domestics by asking their Black comrades if their relatives could work for them. Jones argued that the problems in the Party went beyond a failure to elevate Black women into leadership positions; it also included a dismissal of Black women's labor, a failure to organize them as workers, and an ignorance of racism in its own ranks.

An important, and often ignored, critique that Jones included in her "Neglect" essay was the need for the Party to center Black women leaders in the peace movement. Jones argued that U.S. anti-communism was propagandized as a resistance to authoritarianism, but was in fact fascist authoritarianism under the guise of liberal democracy. This was evidenced in the silencing of the Black Freedom Struggle by targeting its adherents in the CPUSA; it also tempered and constrained the liberal civil rights movement.

Liberal retreat in the face of anti-communism was worrisome; Jones argued that some women's organizations that had been anti-imperialist favored anti-communist policies like the Marshall Plan and Truman Doctrine which obfuscated the reality that the U.S. was fast becoming an economic imperialist behemoth. Anti-communism became the mechanism that allowed the U.S. to violate national sovereignty and undermine liberation movements in the U.S. and Africa, Latin America, and Asia.

Women under fascist states, like the anti-communist state, found their rights further delimited by domestic containment, while Black women were exploited in domestic work where labor unions feared to tread as they were under red-baiting attacks. The U.S. further used anti-communism to justify its neo-colonial extraction of labor and resources abroad, and U.S. intervention in the Korean War proved this for communists. For Jones, this environment amounted to fascism; her vision of peace was of a country and a world without war, but, more than that, she understood that capitalism thrived on war and therefore had to be demolished to create the conditions for emancipation. She would conclude that socialism was the "final and full guarantee" of liberation.

Scholars have recognized that what Jones theorized was like *intersectionality*, but because her theory is grounded in the Marxist-Leninist tradition, James Smethurst describes Jones as the "Black Marxist Feminist ancestor of intersectionality." Jones articulated a different feminism that rejected universalizing women's experiences and the early bourgeois feminist assertions that reduced women and their oppression to essentialist natures. Her analysis was grounded in, but also an expansion of, the Marxist-Leninist canon.

Boyce Davies argues that Jones's assertion of Black women's super-exploitation highlights that they were exploited by others in the working class. John Munro has positioned Jones's argument within her anti-imperialism because she rejected U.S. anti-communism as democratic and highlighted that it justified the U.S.'s anti-democratic incursions overseas. The article was released a full year before U.S. intervention in Korea, but Jones knew that anti-communism justified the exporting of the exploitative conditions under U.S. liberal democracy to other places similarly seeking liberation.[4]

The "Neglect" article has been influential for later generations of activists and scholars who would adopt an intersectional analysis. Scholars argue that the article has influenced leftists' analyses of oppression, becoming a foundation for Black feminism. But some of the challenges

---

    4   James Smethurst, "Claudia Jones, The West Indian Gazette and Afro-Asian Caribbean News and the Rise of a New Black Radicalism in the UK and US," Science & Society, Vol. 87, 2, April 2023, 266; Dr. Carole Boyce Davies and Dr. Charisse Burden-Stelly, "Claudia Jones Research and Collections: Questions of Process and Knowledge Construction," *Journal of Intersectionality*, Vol. 3, 1 (Summer 2019): 6; John Munro, *The Anticolonial Front: The African American Freedom Struggle and Global Decolonization, 1945-1960* (Cambridge: Cambridge University Press, 2017), pp. 123-124.

Jones articulated still remain in the progressive movement today, as U.S. fascism has renewed its assaults on the left.

White chauvinism, Jones argued, manifested among progressives as well as conservatives. White women progressives failed to recognize that Black women's emancipation was essential to their own emancipation. This white chauvinism often emerged as condescension from white colleagues who failed to understand that their racism amounted to complicity with fascists. Despite these shortcomings, Jones believed that a multiracial alliance was the key to mass struggle. Her theoretical work was meant to challenge Party leadership and the rank-and-file to abandon their chauvinism; but, more importantly, to understand that the tools to dismantle oppressive institutions could be leveraged by a coalition devoted to anti-racism, anti-sexism, anti-imperialism, and anti-war.

An End to the Neglect of the Problems of the Negro Woman![1]

1949

Claudia Jones

An outstanding feature of the present stage of the Negro liberation movement is the growth in the militant participation of Negro women in all aspects of the struggle for peace, civil rights, and economic security. Symptomatic of this new militancy is the fact that Negro women have become symbols of many present-day struggles of the Negro people. This growth of militancy among Negro women has profound meaning, both for the Negro liberation movement and for the emerging antifascist, anti-imperialist coalition.

To understand this militancy correctly, to deepen and extend the role of Negro women in the struggle for peace and for all interests of the working class and the Negro people, means primarily to overcome the gross neglect of the special problems of Negro women. This neglect has too long permeated the ranks of the labor movement generally, of Left-progressives, and also of the Communist Party. The most serious assessment of these shortcomings by progressives, especially by Marxist-Leninists, is vitally necessary if we are to help accelerate this development and integrate Negro women in the progressive and labor movement and in our own Party.

The bourgeoisie is fearful of the militancy of the Negro woman, and

---

1   **Ed. Note:** Originally published in *Political Affairs*, June 1949, pp. 51-67.

for good reason. The capitalists know, far better than many progressives seem to know, that once Negro women undertake action, the militancy of the whole Negro people, and thus of the anti-imperialist coalition, is greatly enhanced.

Historically, the Negro woman has been the guardian, the protector, of the Negro family. From the days of the slave traders down to the present, the Negro woman has had the responsibility of caring for the needs of the family, of militantly shielding it from the blows of Jim Crow insults, of rearing children in an atmosphere of lynch terror, segregation, and police brutality, and of fighting for an education for the children. The intensified oppression of the Negro people, which has been the hallmark of the postwar reactionary offensive, cannot therefore but lead to an acceleration of the militancy of the Negro woman. As mother, as Negro, and as worker, the Negro woman fights against the wiping out of the Negro family, against the Jim Crow ghetto existence which destroys the health, morale, and very life of millions of her sisters, brothers, and children.

Viewed in this light, it is not accidental that the American bourgeoisie has intensified its oppression, not only of the Negro people in general, but of Negro women in particular. Nothing so exposes the drive to fascization in the nation as the callous attitude which the bourgeoisie displays and cultivates toward Negro women. The vaunted boast of the ideologists of Big Business—that American women possess "the greatest equality" in the world is exposed in all its hypocrisy when one sees that in many parts of the world, particularly in the Soviet Union, the New Democracies and the formerly oppressed land of China, women are attaining new heights of equality. But above all else, Wall Street's boast stops at the water's edge where Negro and working-class women are concerned. Not equality, but degradation and super-exploitation: this is the actual lot of Negro women!

Consider the hypocrisy of the Truman Administration, which boasts about "exporting democracy throughout the world" while the state of Georgia keeps a widowed Negro mother of twelve children under lock and key. Her crime? She defended her life and dignity-aided by her two sons from the attacks of a "white supremacist." Or ponder the mute silence with which the Department of Justice has greeted Mrs. Amy Mallard, widowed Negro school-teacher, since her husband was lynched in Georgia because he had bought a new Cadillac and became, in the opinion of the "white supremacists," "too uppity." Contrast this with the crocodile tears shed by the U.S. delegation to the United Nations for Cardinal Mindszenty, who collaborated with the enemies of the Hungarian People's Republic and sought to hinder the forward march to fuller democracy by the formerly oppressed workers and peasants of Hungary. Only recently, President Truman spoke solicitously in a Mother's Day Proclamation about the manifestation of "our love and reverence" for all mothers of the land. The so-called "love and reverence" for the mothers of the land by no means includes Negro mothers who, like Rosa Lee Ingram, Amy Mallard, the wives and mothers of the Trenton Six, or the other countless victims, dare to fight back against lynch law and "white supremacy" violence.

Economic Hardships

Very much to the contrary, Negro women—as workers, as Negroes, and as women—are the most oppressed stratum of the whole population. In 1940, two out of every five Negro women, in contrast to two out of every eight white women, worked for a living. By virtue of their majority status among the Negro people, Negro women not only constitute the largest percentage of women heads of families, but are the main breadwinners of the Negro family. The large proportion of Negro women in the labor market is primarily a result of the low-scale earnings of Negro men. This disproportion also has its roots in the treatment and position of Negro women over the centuries.

Following emancipation, and persisting to the present day, a large percentage of Negro women—married as well as single—were forced to work for a living. But despite the shift in employment of Negro women from rural to urban areas, Negro women are still generally confined to the lowest paying jobs. The Women's Bureau, U.S. Department of Labor, *Handbook of Facts for Women Workers* (1948, Bulletin 225), shows white women workers as having median earnings more than twice as high as those of non-white women, and non-white women workers (mainly Negro women) as earning less than $500 a year! In the rural South, the earnings of women are even less. In three large Northern industrial communities, the median income of white families ($1,720) is almost 60 percent higher than that of Negro families ($1,095). The super-exploitation of the Negro woman worker is thus revealed not only in that she receives, as woman, less than equal pay for equal work with men, but in that the majority of Negro women get less than half the pay of white women. Little wonder, then, that in Negro communities the conditions of ghetto-living—low salaries, high rents, high prices, etc.—virtually become an iron curtain hemming in the lives of Negro children and undermining their health and spirit! Little wonder that the maternity death rate for Negro women is triple that of white women! Little wonder that one out of every ten Negro children born in the United States does not grow to manhood or womanhood!

The low scale of earnings of the Negro woman is directly related to her almost complete exclusion from virtually all fields of work except the most menial and underpaid, namely, domestic service. Revealing are the following data given in the report of 1945, *Negro Women War Workers* (Women's Bureau, U.S. Department of Labor, Bulletin 205): out of a total of seven and a half million Negro women, over a million are in domestic and personal service. The overwhelming bulk—about 918,000—of these women workers are employed in private families, and some 98,000 are employed as cooks, waitresses, and in like services in other than private homes. The remaining 60,000 workers in service trades are in miscellaneous personal service occupations (beauticians, boarding house and lodging-house keepers, charwomen, janitors, practical nurses, housekeepers, hostesses, and elevator operators).

The next largest number of Negro women workers are engaged in agricultural work. In 1940, about 245,000 were agricultural workers. Of them, some 128,000 were unpaid family workers. Industrial and other workers numbered more than 96,000 of the Negro women reported. Thirty-six thousand of these women were in manufacturing, the chief groups being 11,300 in apparel and other fabricated textile products, 11,000 in tobacco manufactures, and 5,600 in food and related products.

Clerical and kindred workers in general numbered only 13,000. There were only 8,300 Negro women workers in civil service.

The rest of the Negro women who work for a living were distributed along the following lines: teachers, 50,000; nurses and student nurses, 6,700; social and welfare workers, 1,700; dentists, pharmacists, and veterinarians, 120; physicians and surgeons, 129; actresses, 200; authors, editors, and reporters, 100; lawyers and judges, 39; librarians, 400; and other categories likewise illustrating the large-scale exclusion of Negro women from the professions.

During the anti-Axis war, Negro women for the first time in history had an opportunity to utilize their skills and talents in occupations other than domestic and personal service. They became trailblazers in many fields. Since the end of the war, however, this has given way to growing unemployment, to the wholesale firing of Negro women, particularly in basic industry.

This process has been intensified with the development of the economic crisis. Today, Negro women are being forced back into domestic work in great numbers. In New York State, for example, this trend was officially confirmed recently when Edward Corsi, Commissioner of the State Labor Department, revealed that for the first time since the war, domestic help is readily obtainable. Corsi in effect admitted that Negro women are not voluntarily giving up jobs, but rather are being systematically pushed out of industry. Unemployment, which has always hit the Negro woman first and hardest, plus the high cost of living, is what compels Negro women to re-enter domestic service today. Accompanying this trend is an ideological campaign to make domestic work palatable. Daily newspaper advertisements which base their arguments on the claim that most domestic workers who apply for jobs through U.S.E.S. "prefer this type of work to work in industry," are propagandizing the "virtues" of domestic work, especially of "sleep-in positions."

Inherently connected with the question of job opportunities where the Negro woman is concerned, is the special oppression she faces as Negro, as woman, and as worker. She is the victim of the white chauvinist stereotype as to where her place should be. In the film, radio, and press, the Negro woman is not pictured in her real role as breadwinner, mother, and protector of the family, but as a traditional "mammy" who puts the care of children and families of others above her own. This traditional stereotype of the Negro slave mother, which to this day appears in commercial advertisements, must be combated and rejected as a device of the imperialists to perpetuate the white chauvinist ideology that Negro women are "backward," "inferior," and the "natural slaves" of others.

Historical Aspects

Actually, the history of the Negro woman shows that the Negro mother under slavery held a key position and played a dominant role in her own family grouping. This was due primarily to two factors: the conditions of slavery, under which marriage, as such, was non-existent, and the Negro's social status was derived from the mother and not the father;

and the fact that most of the Negro people brought to these shores by the slave traders came from West Africa where the position of women, based on active participation in property control, was relatively higher in the family than that of European women.

Early historians of the slave trade recall the testimony of travelers indicating that the love of the African mother for her child was unsurpassed in any part of the world. There are numerous stories attesting to the self-sacrificial way in which East African mothers offered themselves to the slave traders in order to save their sons and Hottentot women refused food during famines until after their children were fed.

It is impossible within the confines of this article to relate the terrible sufferings and degradation undergone by Negro mothers arid Negro women generally under slavery. Subject to legalized rape by the slave-owners, confined to slave pens, forced to march for eight to fourteen hours with loads on their backs and to perform back-breaking work even during pregnancy, Negro women bore a burning hatred for slavery, and undertook a large share of the responsibility for defending and nurturing the Negro family.

The Negro mother was mistress in the slave cabin, and despite the interference of master or overseer, her wishes in regard to mating and in family matters were paramount. During and after slavery, Negro women had to support themselves and the children. Necessarily playing an important role in the economic and social life of her people, the Negro woman became schooled in self-reliance, in courageous and selfless action.[2]

There is documentary material of great interest which shows that Negro family life and the social and political consciousness of Negro men and women underwent important changes after emancipation. One freedman observed, during the Civil War, that many men were exceedingly jealous of their newly acquired authority in family relations and insisted upon a recognition of their superiority over women. After the Civil War, the slave rows were broken up and the tenant houses scattered all over the plantation in order that each family might carry on an independent existence. The new economic arrangement, the change in the mode of production, placed the Negro man in a position of authority in relation to his family. Purchase of homesteads also helped strength-

---

2 Today, in the rural sections of the South, especially on the remnants of the old plantations, one finds households where old grandmothers rule their daughters, sons, and grand-children with a matriarchal authority.

en the authority of the male.

Thus, a former slave, who began life as a freedman on a "one-horse" farm, with his wife working as a laundress, but who later rented land and hired two men, recalls the pride which he felt because of his new status: "In my humble palace on a hill in the woods beneath the shade of towering pines and sturdy oaks, I felt as a king whose supreme commands were 'law and gospel' to my subjects."

One must see the double motive was operative here. In regard to his wife and children, the Negro man was now enabled to assume economic and other authority over the family; but he also could fight against violation of women of his group where formerly he was powerless to interfere.

The founding of the Negro church, which from the outset was under the domination of men, also tended to confirm the man's authority in the family. Sanction for male ascendancy was found in the Bible, which for many was the highest authority in such matters.

Through these and other methods, the subordination of Negro women developed. In a few cases, instead of legally emancipating his wife and children, the husband permitted them to continue in their status of slaves. In many cases, state laws forbade a slave emancipated after a certain date to remain in the state. Therefore, the only way for many Negro wives and children to remain in the state was to become "enslaved" to their relatives. Many Negro owners of slaves were really relatives of their slaves.

In some cases, Negro women refused to become subject to the authority of the men. In defiance of the decisions of their husbands to live on the places of their former masters, many Negro women took their children and moved elsewhere.

Negro Women In Mass Organizations

This brief picture of some of the aspects of the history of the Negro woman, seen in the additional light of the fact that a high proportion of Negro women are obliged today to earn all or part of the bread of the family, helps us understand why Negro women play a most active part in the economic, social, and political life of the Negro community today. Approximately 2,500,000 Negro women are organized in social, political, and fraternal clubs and organizations. The most prominent of their organizations are the National Association of Negro women, the National Council of Negro Women, the National Federation of Women's Clubs, the Women's Division of the Elks' Civil Liberties Committee, the National Association of Colored Beauticians, National Negro Business Women's League, and the National Association of Colored Graduate Nurses. Of these, the National Association of Negro Women, with 75,000 members, is the largest membership organization. There are numerous sororities, church women's committees of all denominations, as well as organizations among women of West Indian descent. In some areas, N.A.A.C.P. chapters have Women's Divisions, and recently the National Urban League established a Women's Division for the first time in its history.

Negro women are the real active forces—the organizers and workers—in all the institutions and organizations of the Negro people. These organizations play a many-sided role, concerning themselves with all questions pertaining to the economic, political, and social life of the Negro people, and particularly of the Negro family. Many of these organizations are intimately concerned with the problems of Negro youth, in the form of providing and administering educational scholarships, giving assistance to schools and other institutions, and offering community service. The fight for higher education in order to break down Jim Crow in higher institutions was symbolized last year, by the brilliant Negro woman student, Ada Lois Sipuel Fisher of Oklahoma. The disdainful attitudes which are sometimes expressed—that Negro women's organizations concern themselves only with "charity" work—must be exposed as of chauvinist derivation, however subtle, because while the same could be said of many organizations of white women, such attitudes fail to recognize the special character of the role of Negro women's organizations. This approach, fails to recognize the special function which Negro women play in these organizations, which, over and above their particular function, seek to provide social services denied to Negro youth as a result of the Jim Crow lynch system in the U.S.

The Negro Woman Worker

The negligible participation of Negro women in progressive and trade-union circles is thus all the more startling. In union after union, even in those unions where a large concentration of workers are Negro women, few Negro women are to be found as leaders or active workers. The outstanding exceptions to this are the Food and Tobacco Workers' Union and the United Office and Professional Workers' Union.

But why should these be exceptions? Negro women are among the most militant trade unionists. The sharecroppers' strikes of the '30s were sparkplugged by Negro women. Subject to the terror of the landlord and white supremacist, they waged magnificent battles together with Negro men and white progressives in that struggle of great tradition led by the Communist Party. Negro women played a magnificent part in the pre-C.I.O. days in strikes and other struggles, both as workers and as wives of workers, to win recognition of the principle of industrial unionism, in such industries as auto, packing, steel, etc. More recently, the militancy of Negro women unionists is shown in the strike of the packinghouse workers, and even more so, in the tobacco workers' strike—in which such leaders as Moranda Smith and Velma Hopkins emerged as outstanding trade unionists. The struggle of the tobacco workers led by Negro women later merged with the political action of Negro and white which led to the election of the first Negro in the South (in Winston Salem, N. C.) since Reconstruction days.

It is incumbent on progressive unionists to realize that in the fight for equal rights for Negro workers, it is necessary to have a special approach to Negro women workers, who, far out of proportion to other women workers, are the main breadwinners in their families. The fight to retain the Negro woman in industry and to upgrade her on the job, is a major way of struggling for the basic and special interests of the Negro woman worker. Not to recognize this feature is to miss the special aspects of the effects of the growing economic crisis, which is penalizing Negro workers, particularly Negro women workers, with special severity.

The Domestic Worker

One of the crassest manifestations of trade-union neglect of the problems of the Negro woman worker has been the failure, not only to fight against relegation of the Negro woman to domestic and similar menial work, but to organize the domestic worker. It is merely lip service for progressive unionists to speak of organizing the unorganized without turning their eyes to the serious plight of the domestic worker, who, unprotected by union standards, is also the victim of exclusion from all social and labor legislation. Only about one in ten of all Negro women workers is covered by present minimum-wage legislation, although about one-fourth of all such workers are to be found in states having minimum-wage laws. All of the arguments heretofore projected with regard to the real difficulties of organizing the domestic workers—such as the "casual" nature of their employment, the difficulties of organizing day workers, the problem of organizing people who work in individual households, etc.,—must be overcome forthwith. There is a danger that Social-Democratic forces may enter this field to do their work of spreading disunity and demagogy, unless progressives act quickly.

The lot of the domestic worker is one of unbearable misery. Usually, she has no definition of tasks in the household where she works. Domestic workers may have "thrown in," in addition to cleaning and scrubbing, such tasks as washing windows, caring for the children, laundering, cooking, etc., and all at the lowest pay. The Negro domestic worker must suffer the additional indignity, in some areas, of having to seek work in virtual "slave markets" on the streets where bids are made, as from a slave block, for the hardiest workers. Many a domestic worker, on returning to her own household, must begin housework anew to keep her own family together.

Who was not enraged when it was revealed in California, in the heinous case of Dora Jones, that a Negro woman domestic was enslaved for more than 40 years in "civilized" America? Her "employer" was given a minimum sentence of a few years and complained that the sentence was for "such a long period of time." But could Dora Jones, Negro domestic worker, be repaid for more than 40 years of her life under such conditions of exploitation and degradation? And how many cases, partaking in varying degrees of the condition of Dora Jones, are still tolerated by progressives themselves!

Only recently, in the New York State Legislature, legislative proposals were made to "fingerprint" domestic workers. The Martinez Bill did not see the light of day, because the reactionaries were concentrating on other repressive legislative measures; but here we see clearly the imprint of the African "pass" system of British imperialism (and of the German Reich in relation to the Jewish people!) being attempted in relation to women domestic workers.

It is incumbent on the trade unions to assist the Domestic Workers' Union in every possible way to accomplish the task of organizing the exploited domestic workers, the majority of whom are Negro women. Simultaneously, a legislative fight for the inclusion of domestic workers under the benefits of the Social Security Law is vitally urgent and necessary. Here, too, recurrent questions regarding "administrative problems" of applying the law to domestic workers should be challenged and solutions found.

The continued relegation of Negro women to domestic work has helped to perpetuate and intensify chauvinism directed against all Negro women. Despite the fact that Negro women may be grandmothers or mothers, the use of the chauvinist term "girl" for adult Negro women is a common expression. The very economic relationship of Negro women to white women, which perpetuates "madam-maid" relationships, feeds chauvinist attitudes and makes it incumbent on white women progressives, and particularly Communists, to fight consciously against all manifestations of white chauvinism, open and subtle.

Chauvinism on the part of progressive white women is often expressed in their failure to have close ties of friendship with Negro women and to realize that this fight for equality of Negro women is in their own self-interest, inasmuch as the super-exploitation and oppression of Negro women tends to depress the standards of all women. Too many progressives, and even some Communists, are still guilty of exploiting Negro domestic workers, of refusing to hire them through the Domestic Workers' Union (or of refusing to help in its expansion into those areas where it does not yet exist), and generally of participating in the vilification of "maids" when speaking to their bourgeois neighbors and their own families. Then, there is the expressed "concern" that the exploited Negro domestic worker does not "talk" to, or is not "friendly" with, her employer, or the habit of assuming that the duty of the white progressive employer is to "inform" the Negro woman of her exploitation and her oppression which she undoubtedly knows quite intimately. Persistent challenge to every chauvinist remark as concerns the Negro woman is vitally necessary, if we are to break down the understandable distrust on the part of Negro women who are repelled by the white chauvinism they often find expressed in progressive circles.

Manifestations Of White Chauvinism

Some of the crassest expressions of chauvinism are to be found at social affairs, where, all too often, white men and women and Negro men participate in dancing, but Negro women are neglected. The acceptance of white ruling-class standards of "desirability" for women (such as light skin), the failure to extend courtesy to Negro women and to integrate Negro women into organizational leadership, are other forms of chauvinism.

Another rabid aspect of the Jim Crow oppression of the Negro woman is expressed in the numerous laws which are directed against her as regards property rights, inter-marriage (originally designed to prevent white men in the South from marrying Negro women), and laws which hinder and deny the right of choice, not only to Negro women, but Negro and white men and women.

For white progressive women and men, and especially for Communists, the question of social relations with Negro men and women is above all a question of strictly adhering to social equality. This means ridding ourselves of the position which sometimes finds certain progressives and Communists fighting on the economic and political issues facing the Negro people, but "drawing the line" when it come to social intercourse or inter-marriage. To place the question as a "personal" and not a political matter, when such questions arise, is to be guilty of the worst kind of Social-Democratic, bourgeois-liberal thinking as regard the Negro question in American life; it is to be guilty of imbibing the poisonous white-chauvinist "theories" of a Bilbo or a Rankin. Similarly, too, with regard to guaranteeing the "security" of children. This security will be enhanced only through the struggle for the liberation and equality of all nations and peoples, and not by shielding children from the knowledge of this struggle. This means ridding ourselves of the bourgeois-liberal attitudes which "permit" Negro and white children of progressives to play together at camps when young, but draw the line when the children reach teen-age and establish boy-girl relationships.

The bourgeois ideologists have not failed, of course, to develop a special ideological offensive aimed at degrading Negro women, as part and parcel of the general reactionary ideological offensive against women of "kitchen, church, and children." They cannot, however, with equanimity or credibility, speak of the Negro woman's "place" as in the home; for Negro women are in other peoples' kitchens. Hence, their task has been to intensify their theories of male "superiority" as regards the Negro woman by developing introspective attitudes which coincide with the "new school" of "psychological inferiority" of women. The whole intent of a host of articles, books, etc., has been to obscure the main responsibility for the oppression of Negro women by spreading the rotten bourgeois notion about a "battle of the sexes" and "ignoring" the fight of both Negro men and women—the whole Negro people—against their common oppressors, the white ruling class.

Chauvinist expressions also include paternalistic surprise when it is learned that Negroes are professional people. Negro professional women workers are often confronted with such remarks as "Isn't your family proud of you?" Then, there is the reverse practice of inquiring of Negro women professionals whether "someone in the family" would like to take a job as a domestic worker.

The responsibility for overcoming these special forms of white chauvinism rests, not with the "subjectivity" of Negro women, as it is often put, but squarely on the shoulders of white men and white women. Negro men have a special responsibility particularly in relation to rooting out attitudes of male superiority as regards women in general.

There is need to root out all "humanitarian" and patronizing attitudes toward Negro women. In one community, a leading Negro trade unionist, the treasurer of her Party section, would be told by a white progressive woman after every social function: "Let me have the money; something may happen to you." In another instance, a Negro domestic worker who wanted to join the Party was told by her employer, a Communist, that she was "too backward" and "wasn't ready" to join the Party. In yet another community, which since the war has been populated in the proportion of sixty per cent Negro to forty per cent white, white progressive mothers maneuvered to get their children out of the school in this community. To the credit of the initiative of the Party section organizer, a Negro woman, a struggle was begun which forced a change in arrangements which the school principal, yielding to the mothers' and to his own prejudices, had established. These arrangements involved a special class in which a few white children were isolated with "selected Negro kids" in what was termed an "experimental class in race relations."

These chauvinist attitudes, particularly as expressed toward the Negro woman, are undoubtedly an important reason for the grossly insufficient participation of Negro women in progressive organizations and in our Party as members and leaders.

The American bourgeoisie, we must remember, is aware of the present and even greater potential role of the masses of Negro women, and is therefore not loathe to throw plums to Negroes who betray their people and do the bidding of imperialism.

Faced with the exposure of their callous attitude to Negro women, faced with the growing protests against unpunished lynchings and the legal lynchings "Northern style," Wall Street is giving a few token positions to Negro women. Thus, Anna Arnold Hedgeman, who played a key role in the Democratic National Negro Committee to Elect Truman, was rewarded with the appointment as Assistant to Federal Security Administrator Ewing. Thus, too, Governor Dewey appointed Irene Diggs to a high post in the New York State Administration.

Another straw in the wind showing attempts to whittle down the militancy of Negro women was the State Department's invitation to a representative of the National Council of Negro Women—the only Negro organization so designated—to witness the signing of the Atlantic Pact.

Key Issues Of Struggle

There are many key issues facing Negro women around which struggles can and must be waged.

But none so dramatizes the oppressed status of Negro womanhood as does the case of Rosa Lee Ingram, widowed Negro mother of fourteen children—two of them dead—who faces life imprisonment in a Georgia jail for the "crime" of defending herself from the indecent advances of a "white supremacist." The Ingram case illustrates the landless, Jim Crow, oppressed status of the Negro family in America. It illumines particularly the degradation of Negro women today under American bourgeois democracy moving to fascism and war. It reflects the daily insults to which Negro women are subjected in public places, no matter what their class, status, or position. It exposes the hypocritical alibi of the lynchers of Negro manhood who have historically hidden behind the skirts of white women when they try to cover up their foul crimes with the "chivalry" of "protecting white womanhood." But white women, today, no less than their sisters in the abolitionist and suffrage movements, must rise to challenge this lie and the whole system of Negro oppression.

American history is rich in examples of the cost—to the democratic rights of both women and men—of failure to wage this fight. The suffragists, during their first jailings, were purposely placed on cots next to Negro prostitutes to "humiliate" them. They had the wisdom to understand that the intent was to make it so painful, that no women would dare to fight for her rights if she had to face such consequences. But it was the historic shortcoming of the women's suffrage leaders, predominantly drawn as they were from the bourgeoisie and the petty-bourgeoisie, that they failed to link their own struggles to the struggles for the full democratic rights of the Negro people following emancipation.

A developing consciousness on the woman question today, therefore, must not fail to recognize that the Negro question in the United States is *prior* to, and not equal to, the woman question; that only to the extent that we fight all chauvinist expressions and actions as regards the Negro people and fight for the full equality of the Negro people, can women as a whole advance their struggle for equal rights. For the progressive women's movement, the Negro woman, who combines in her status the worker, the Negro, and the woman, is the vital link to this heightened political consciousness. To the extent, further, that the cause of the Negro woman worker is promoted, she will be enabled to take her rightful place in the Negro proletarian leadership of the national liberation movement, and by her active participation contribute to the entire American working class, whose historic mission is the achievement of a Socialist America—the final and full guarantee of woman's emancipation.

The fight for Rosa Lee Ingram's freedom is a challenge to all white women and to all progressive forces, who must begin to ask themselves: How long shall we allow this dastardly crime against all womenhood, against the Negro people, to go unchallenged! Rosa Lee Ingram's plight and that of her sisters also carries with it a challenge to progressive cultural workers to write and sing of the Negro woman in her full courage and dignity.

The recent establishment of the National Committee to Free the Ingram Family fulfills a need long felt since the early movement which forced commutation to life imprisonment of Mrs. Ingram's original sentence of execution. This National Committee, headed by Mary Church Terrell, a founder of the National Association of Colored Women, includes among its leaders such prominent women, Negro and white, as Therese Robinson, National Grand Directoress of the Civil Liberties Committee of the Elks, Ada B. Jackson, and Dr. Gene Weltfish.

One of the first steps of the Committee was the visit of a delegation of Negro and white citizens to this courageous, militant Negro mother imprisoned in a Georgia cell. The measure of support was so great that the Georgia authorities allowed the delegation to see her unimpeded. Since that time, however, in retaliation against the developing mass movement, the Georgia officials have moved Mrs. Ingram, who is suffering from a severe heart condition, to a worse penitentiary, at Reedsville.

Support to the work of this committee becomes a prime necessity for all progressives, particularly women. President Truman must be stripped of his pretense of "know-nothing" about the Ingram case. To free the Ingrams, support must be rallied for the success of the million-signatures campaign, and for U.N. action on the Ingram brief soon to be filed.

The struggle for jobs for Negro women is a prime issue. The growing economic crisis, with its mounting unemployment and wage-cuts and increasing evictions, is making its impact felt most heavily on the Negro masses. In one Negro community after another, Negro women, the last to be hired and the first to be fired, are the greatest sufferers from unemployment. Struggles must be developed to win jobs for Negro women in basic industry, in the white-collar occupations, in the communities, and in private utilities.

The successful campaign of the Communist Party in New York's East Side to win jobs for Negro women in the five-and-dime stores has led to the hiring of Negro women throughout the city, even in predominantly white communities. This campaign has extended to New England and must be waged elsewhere. Close to 15 government agencies do not hire Negroes at all. This policy gives official sanction to, and at the same time further encourages, the pervasive Jim Crow policies of the capitalist exploiters. A campaign to win jobs for Negro women here would thus greatly advance the whole struggle for jobs for Negro men and women. In addition, it would have a telling effect in exposing the hypocrisy of the Truman Administration's "Civil Rights" program.

A strong fight will also have to be made against the growing practice of the United States Employment Service to shunt Negro women, despite their qualifications for other jobs, only into domestic and personal service work.

Where consciousness of the special role of Negro women exists, successful struggle can be initiated which will win the support of white workers. A recent example was the initiative taken by white Communist garment workers in a shop employing 25 Negro women where three machines were idle. The issue of upgrading Negro women workers became a vital one. A boycott movement has been initiated and the machines stand unused as of this writing, the white workers refusing to adhere to strict seniority at the expense of Negro workers. Meanwhile, negotiations are continuing on this issue. Similarly, in a Packard U.A.W. local in Detroit, a fight for the maintenance of women in industry and for the upgrading of 750 women, the large majority of whom were Negro, was recently won.

The Struggle For Peace

Winning the Negro women for the struggle for peace is decisive for all other struggles. Even during the anti-Axis war, Negro women had to weep for their soldier-sons, lynched while serving in a Jim Crow army. Are they, therefore, not interested in the struggle for peace?

The efforts of the bipartisan war makers to gain the support of the women's organizations in general, have influenced many Negro women's organizations, which, at their last annual conventions, adopted foreign-policy stands favoring the Marshall Plan and Truman Doctrine. Many of these organizations have worked with groups having outspoken anti-imperialist positions.

That there is profound peace sentiment among Negro women which can be mobilized for effective action is shown, not only in the magnificent response to the meetings of Eslande Goode Robeson, but also in the position announced last year by the oldest Negro women's organization, under the leadership of Mrs. Christine C. Smith, in urging a national mobilization of American Negro women in support of the United Nations. In this connection, it will be very fruitful to bring to our country a consciousness of the magnificent struggles of women in North Africa, who, though lacking in the most elementary material needs, have organized a strong movement for peace and thus stand united against a Third World War, with 81 million women in 57 nations, in the Women's International Democratic Federation.

Our Party, based on its Marxist-Leninist principles, stands foursquare on a program of full economic, political, and social equality for the Negro people and of equal rights for women. Who, more than the Negro woman, the most exploited and oppressed, belongs in our Party? Negro women can and must make an enormous contribution to the daily life and work of the Party. Concretely, this means prime responsibility lies with white men and women comrades. Negro men comrades, however, must participate in this task. Negro Communist women must everywhere now take their rightful place in Party leadership on all levels.

The strong capacities, militancy and organizational talents of Negro women, can, if well utilized by our Party, be a powerful lever for bringing forward Negro workers—men and women—as the leading forces of the Negro people's liberation movement for cementing Negro and Wall Street imperialism, and for rooting the Party among the most exploited and oppressed sections of the working class and its allies.

In our Party clubs, we must conduct an intensive discussion of the role of the Negro women, so as to equip our Party membership with clear understanding for undertaking the necessary struggles in the shops and communities. We must end the practice, in which many Negro women who join our Party, and who, in their churches, communities and fraternal groups are leaders of masses, with an invaluable mass experience to give to our Party, suddenly find themselves viewed in our clubs, not as leaders, but as people who have "to get their feet wet" organizationally. We must end this failure to create an atmosphere in our clubs in which new recruits—in this case Negro women—are confronted with the "silent treatment" or with attempts to "blueprint" them into a pattern. In addition to the white chauvinist implications in such approaches, these practices confuse the basic need for Marxist-Leninist understanding which our Party gives to all workers, and which enhances their political understanding, with chauvinist disdain for the organizational talents of new Negro members, or for the necessity to promote them into leadership.

To win the Negro women for full participation in the anti-fascist, anti-imperialist coalition, to bring her militancy and participation to even greater heights in the current and future struggles against Wall Street imperialism, progressives must acquire political consciousness as regards her special oppressed status.

It is this consciousness, accelerated by struggles, that will convince increasing thousands that only the Communist Party, as the vanguard of the working class, with its ultimate perspective of Socialism, can achieve for the Negro women—for the entire Negro people—the full equality and dignity of their stature in a Socialist society in which contributions to society are measured, not by national origin, or by color, but a society in which men and women contribute according to ability, and ultimately under Communism receive according to their needs.

Theoretical Foundations 39

CLAUDIA JONES, a dedicated member of the CPUSA, Black nationalist, and feminist, devoted her efforts to establishing a broad, intersectional, anti-imperialist coalition led by working-class leadership and driven by women's active participation. Jones tirelessly advocated for equal respect for Black women within the Party, striving to empower women as mothers, workers, individuals, and organizers. Jones' campaigns encompassed a wide range of issues, from job training programs and equal pay for women to government controls on food prices and funding for wartime childcare. Jones championed women's rights through subcommittees, theoretical training, mass organizations, daytime classes, and babysitter funds, leaving an indelible mark on the party's commitment to gender equality, and to anti-imperialist struggles abroad.

SECTION 3
ANTI-IMPERIALISM AT THE HEIGHT OF THE ANTI-COMMUNIST WITCH HUNT

International Women's Day as a New Day against Imperialism[1]

Liberation School

In an article published for International Women's Day [IWD] 2023, Maddie Dery summarizes the various experiences of the women's liberation movement since the early 20th century: "The history of International Women's Day teaches us that when we fight, we win."[2] This spirit, which threads through the historic struggle for women's liberation and socialism, is easily identified in the revolutionary origins, legacies, and futures of International Women's Day and can also be found in Claudia Jones' historic 1950 speech at an International Women's Day rally, which was also published in *Political Affairs*, the monthly journal of the Communist Party USA (CPUSA). Jones' speech, which follows this article, rooted the contemporary moment of the class struggle in the long history of the fight for Black liberation, women's emancipation, peace, and socialism, linking together fighters from Harriet Tubman and Sojourner Truth to Mother Jones and Elizabeth Gurley Flynn, from Lucy Stone and Ida B. Wells to Williana Burroughs and Clara Zetkin.

Born in Trinidad in 1915, Claudia Jones moved to New York City eight years later.[3] She is one of the most significant revolutionary theo-

---

1   **Ed. Note:** This is a modified version of the article "International Women's Day and the Struggle for Peace" that was published by Liberation School on March 29th, 2023. The original article can be accessed at https://www.liberationschool.org/claudia-jones-1950-iwd-speech/

2   Maddie Dery, "This year, IWD means building an anti-imperialist movement," *Breaking the Chains*, 07 March 2023.

3   Adiah Hicks, "Claudia Jones: Revolutionary Feminist and Fighter," *Breaking*

rists and organizers of the 20th century. After joining the Communist Party in 1936 through the struggle to free the Scottsboro Boys,[4] she rapidly developed as an organizer and intellectual and within two years was the associate editor of the CPUSA's *Weekly Review* and after another two years was the lead editor.

Claudia's activism and writings were pushing the Party to prioritize struggles against male and national chauvinism, and, in the late 1940s, Jones theorized the "super-exploitation" of Black working-class women through their structural location in U.S. society. In her 1949 "Neglect" article, she wrote that "the Negro woman, who combines in her status the worker, the Negro, and the woman, is the vital link to [...] heightened political consciousness."[5] For Jones, the heightened oppression of Black women workers and their historic roles as leaders and organizers of their communities made Black women's participation and leadership essential to the communist and progressive struggle.

At the time of her IWD speech, she was solidly recognized as a leading Party and movement intellectual. In addition to her organizing and editorial work, she was elected to the CPUSA's National Committee in 1945. In this speech, she insists on building broad and international unity against U.S. imperialist wars, unity that the Party could only forge by fighting against national, racial, and gender chauvinism. She centers the need for international and broad unity against U.S. militarism and highlighted how IWD isn't only a day to advance the struggle for women, but for all oppressed people. In the U.S., she states, "a fundamental condition for rallying the masses of American women into the peace camp is to free them from the influence of the agents of imperialism and to arouse their sense of internationalism with millions upon millions of their sisters the world over."[6] The heroic struggles of women through-

---

the Chains, 27 December 2018.

4   **Ed. Note:** The Scottsboro boys were a group of 9 Black male teenagers, who were falsely accused and convicted by an all-white jury in an Alabama court. The case became a famous civil rights campaign and their defense was assisted by the CPUSA and NAACP. Though sentenced to death, vigorous solidarity campaigns led to their sentences being appealed and overturned or commuted, however all served extended sentences in various prisons. Their convictions were eventually pardoned, with the last pardons being issued posthumously in 2013.

5   Claudia Jones, "An End to the Neglect of the Problems of the Negro Woman!" *Political Affairs* 28, no. 6 (1949) [see this volume, p. 35].

6   Claudia Jones, "International Women's Day and the Struggle for Peace" *Political Affairs* 29, no. 3 (1950) [see this volume, p. 48].

out the socialist and anti-colonial states in Europe, Asia, and Africa, she held, resulted in "significant anti-imperialist advances" because they were the product of united fronts. As a result, these struggles "should serve to inspire the growing struggles of American women and heighten their consciousness of the need for militant united-front campaigns around the burning demands of the day, against monopoly oppression, against war and fascism."[7]

In the speech below, and in her writing and organizing, she critically assessed her Party's attention to national chauvinism and sexism by recommending concrete actions. Jones called on "progressive and communist men" to "become vanguard fighters against male supremacist ideas and for equal rights for women."[8] In the concluding section of the speech, Jones declares "tremendous tasks fall upon our Party," from deploying Black women leaders to engage mass women's organizing, promoting Black women "in all spheres of Party work and mass activity," engaging in education and study about women's labor—including domestic labor—and insisting that all Party outlets deal explicitly with these matters, for these are the only ways to combat "bourgeois feminism."[9]

As a Black communist and immigrant woman living in the U.S. without citizenship rights during the height of the anti-communist Cold War hysteria, Jones was uniquely vulnerable to state repression. Along with other leading members of the CPUSA, she was subject to heavy surveillance. In January 1948, she was arrested for violating the McCarran Act and was later convicted for violating the 1918 Immigration Act. Held at Ellis Island awaiting deportation, the American Committee for the Protection of the Foreign Born raised her $1,000 bail. Although she was still facing deportation proceedings, Jones didn't back down after her release. She dove right back into organizing, published several key articles on super-exploitation, among other work. Even though her deportation proceedings started in the middle of February 1950, less than a month later Jones delivered the speech reproduced below.

In late June 1951, the state arrested Jones and over a dozen other Party leaders (including her friend Flynn) under the anti-communist Smith Act.[10] The arrest occurred almost immediately after the Supreme Court

---

7   Ibid. [see this volume, p. 49].
8   Ibid. [see this volume, p. 59].
9   Ibid. [see this volume, p. 59].
10 **Ed. Note:** The Smith Act, or Alien Registration Act 1940, was a United

upheld the constitutionality of the Smith Act in *Eugene Dennis v. United States*. At the March 1953 conclusion of the trial she was sentenced to a year and a day in prison. She started serving her sentence in 1955, after the Supreme Court refused to hear her appeal, despite a significant campaign waged outside prison walls by her comrades and friends.

As Carole Boyce Davies' evaluation of Jones' FBI file demonstrates, it was "the cumulative body of her writings that provided the documentary evidence the state used to argue for her deportation," the penalty for her crime of "practicing the ideas of communism."[11] Nonetheless, one of these documents that prompted the arrest was her speech below. In her pre-sentencing remarks before Judge Edward Dimock convicted Jones, she condemned the sham trial and showed the cowardice of the state. "Introduce a title page to show Claudia once wrote an article during the indictment period," she said, "but you dare not read even a line of it, even to a biased jury [...] You dare not, gentlemen of the prosecution, assert that Negro women can think and speak and write!"[12] She continued with reference to her IWD article:

> The prosecution also canceled out the overt act which accompanied the original indictment of the defendant Jones entitled 'Women in the Struggle for Peace and Security.' And why, your Honor? It cannot be read, your Honor—it urges American mothers, Negro women and white, to write, to emulate the peace struggles of their anti-fascist sisters in Latin America, in the new European democracies, in the Soviet Union, in Asia and Africa to end the bestial Korean war.[13]

In an interview after she arrived in Britain, she articulated several reasons she was a threat to the U.S. state:

> I was deported from the USA because as a Negro woman Communist of West Indian descent, I was a thorn in their side in my opposition to Jim Crow racist discrimination against 16 million Negro Americans... my work for re-

---

States federal statute which penalized activities that were perceived as intending to subvert or overthrow the U.S. government, particularly targeting those who weren't naturalized U.S. citizens. Conviction could result in fines, prison sentences, and/or deportation. This Act targeted many socialists and communists, and 9 CPUSA leaders were targeted, tried, and convicted in 1949, with others to follow.

11   Carole Boyce Davies, *Left of Karl Marx: The Political Life of Black Communist Claudia Jones* (Durham: Duke University Press, 2008), 151, 141.

12   Claudia Jones "Claudia Jones," in *13 Communists Speak to the Court* (New York: New Century Publishers, 1953), 22.

13   Ibid., 23.

dress of these grievances, for unity of Negro and white workers, for women's rights... because I fought for peace [...] because I urged the prosecution of lynchers rather than prosecution of Communists and other democratic Americans who oppose the lynchers and big financiers and warmongers, the real advocates of force and violence in the USA.[14]

During the height of Cold War anti-communist witch hunts, Charisse Burden-Stelly writes, "the West Indian's embodied foreignness and internationalism, and the U.S. Black radical's 'foreign' and internationalist ideas, constituted a particular threat that was incompatible with loyalty to the United States." As such, they "were particularly targeted because a multitude of Blacks in the Communist Party of the United States of America (CPUSA), starting in the 1920s, were West Indian workers that analyzed the struggle of the U.S. Black working class as part of the larger fight of the international racialized proletariat against capitalist imperialism and coloniality."[15]

The ruling class always tries to defang the radical foundations of events such as International Women's Day and Women's History Month, deploying them in the exact opposite direction of their real origins and legacy. In 2023, for example, U.S. President Joe Biden even had the nerve to use International Women's Day to launch a broad propaganda campaign to support U.S. imperialist wars and plots against Iran, Russia, Afghanistan, and Ukraine.[16] The real spirit of International Women's Day is what Jones relays in her speech. It is one that is resolutely opposed to imperialism and capitalism, sexism, racism, and national chauvinism, and affirms that those systems of exploitation and oppression can only be eliminated through the struggle for socialism, a struggle that requires uniting the broadest masses of working and oppressed people. This is the spirit in which we continue our struggle for the liberation of Black working women and all exploited and oppressed people.

---

14   Claudia Jones, cited in Davies, *Left of Karl Marx*, 143-144.

15   Charisse Burden-Stelly, "Constructing Deportable Subjectivity: Antiforeignness, Antiradicalism, and Antiblackness during the McCarthyist Structure of Feeling," *Souls* 19, no. 3 (2017): 343.

16   "Biden Criticizes Conditions in Afghanistan, Ukraine on International Women's Day," *The Hill*, 08 March 2023.

International Women's Day and the Struggle for Peace[1]
1950

Claudia Jones

On International Women's Day this year, millions of women in the world-wide camp of peace headed by the mighty land of Socialism will muster their united forces to make March 8, 1950, a day of demonstrative struggle for peace, freedom, and women's rights.

In our own land, there will be over fifty celebrations. On New York's Lower East Side, original site of this historic American-born day of struggle for equal rights for women, and in major industrial states, such as Illinois, Ohio, Michigan, Pennsylvania, California, Massachusetts, and Connecticut, broad united-front meetings of women for peace will be head. "Save the Peace!" "Halt Production of the A-Bomb!" "Negotiate with the Soviet Union to Outlaw Atomic Weapons!"—these are the slogans of women in the U.S.A. on International Women's Day.

The Struggle for Peace

The special significance of this holiday this year, its particular meaning for labor, progressives, and Communists, and for American working women generally, is to be found in the widespread condemnation, among numerous sections of the American people, of Truman's

---

1   **Ed. Note:** Originally published in *Political Affairs*, March 1950, p. 32-45.

cold-blooded order to produce the hydrogen bomb and to inaugurate a suicidal atomic and hydrogen weapon race.

Not to the liking of the imperialist ideologists of the "American Century" is the growing indication by millions of American women of their opposition to war, their ardent desire for peace, their rejection of the Truman-bipartisan war policy.

As in the Protestant women's groups, many women's organizations are opposed to the North Atlantic war pact, which spells misery for the masses of American women and their families. This development coincides with the policy stand of progressive women's organizations that have been outspoken in demands for peaceful negotiations of differences with the Soviet Union, for the outlawing of atomic weapons, for ending the cold war.

Typical of the shocked reaction to Truman's order for H-bomb production was the statement of the Women's International League for Peace and Freedom demanding that Secretary of State Dean Acheson "make clear by action as well as by words that the United States desires negotiations and agreement" with the Soviet Union. This is necessary, the statement added, to avoid "bringing down upon this nation the condemnation of the world." This organization also expressed its opposition to Acheson's suggestion for the resumption of diplomatic relations between U.N. members and Franco-Spain, as well as to the proposed extension of the peace-time draft law.

These and other expressions of opposition to the Administration's H-bomb policy by notable women's organizations and leaders merge with the significant grass-roots united-front peace activities developing in many communities. For example, in Boston, as result of a "Save the Peace—Outlaw the A-Bomb" peace ballot circulated last November, a permanent broad united-front women's organization, "Minute Women for Peace," has been established. In that city, within ten days, over 6,000 women from church, trade-union, fraternal, Negro, civic and middle-class-led women's organizations signed peace ballots urging outlawing of the A-Bomb. In Philadelphia, a Women's Committee For Peace has addressed to President Truman a ballot to "Outlaw the H-Bomb—Vote for Peace." Similar developments have taken place in Pasadena and Chicago. The wide response of women of all political opinions to these ballots is but an index of the readiness of American women to challenge the monstrous Truman-Acheson doctrine that war is inevitable. Emulation of these developments in other cities, particularly among working-class and Negro women, is certainly on the order of the day.

Indicative of the determination of women, not only to register their peace sentiments, but to fight for peace, is the coalescing on a community basis, following such ballotings, of women's peace committees. The orientation of these committees is to convene women's peace conferences, in alliance with the general peace movement now developing.

The widespread peace sentiments, particularly of the women and the youth in their millions, must be organized and given direction and effective, militant expression. This is necessary, since the monopolist rulers are doing everything possible to deceive the people to paralyze their will to fight for peace. Particularly insidious agents of the war-makers are the Social-Democratic and reformist labor leaders, the reactionary Roman Catholic hierarchy, and the American agents of the fascist Tito gang of imperialist spies,[2] whose main task is to confuse, split and undermine the peace camp.

Hence, a fundamental condition for rallying the masses of American women into the peace camp is to free them from the influence of the agents of imperialism and to arouse their sense of internationalism with millions upon millions of their sisters the world over; to protest the repressive and death-dealing measures carried through against the countless women victims by Wall Street's puppets in Marshall-ized Italy, in fascist Greece and Spain; to link them in solidarity with the anti-imperialist women united 80 million strong in 59 lands in the Women's International Democratic Federation, who are in the front ranks of the struggle for peace and democracy.

In these lands, anti-fascist women collect millions of signatures for the outlawing of the A-bomb, against the Marshall Plan and Atlantic war pact, for world disarmament, etc. In the German Democratic Republic, five million signatures were collected by women for outlawing the A-bomb. In Italy, the Union of Italian Women collected more than 2 million such signatures for presentation to the De Gasperi government. In France, women conducted demonstrations when bodies of dead French soldiers were returned to their shores as a result of the Marshall-Plan-financed war of their own government against the heroic

---

2   **Ed. Note:** Following the fallout of the Second World War, disagreements between the Soviet-led bloc of Socialist nations and Tito's Yugoslavia had formed, with accusations of complicity with imperialism and fascism being thrown in both directions between the nations. CPUSA at this time followed the USSR's line on the disagreement.

Vietnamese. In Africa, women barricaded the roads with their bodies to prevent their men from being carted away as prisoners in a militant strike struggle charged with slogans of anti-colonialism and peace. And who can measure the capitalist fear of emulation by American Negro and white women of these peace struggles, particularly of the women of China (as reflected in the All-Asian Women's Conference held last December in Peking), whose feudal bonds were severed forever as a result of the major victory of the Chinese people's revolution?

These and other significant anti-imperialist advances, achieved in united-front struggle, should serve to inspire the growing struggles of American women and heighten their consciousness of the need for militant united-front campaigns around the burning demands of the day, against monopoly oppression, against war and fascism.

Reaction's Ideological and Political Attacks Against Women

American monopoly capital can offer the masses of American women, who compose more than one-half of our country's population, a program only of war and fascism. Typical of the ideology governing this war perspective was the article in the recent mid-century issue of Life magazine entitled "Fifty Years of American Women."

That "contribution" did not hold out the promise to American women along the demagogic 2000 A.D. line of Truman's State of the Union annual message, but brazenly offered the fascist triple-K (*Kinder-Küche-Kirche*) pattern of war and a "war psychology" for American women!

The author, Winthrop Sargeant, drawing upon the decadent, Nazi-adopted "theorist," Oswald Spengler, propounded his cheap philosophy on the expensive Luce paper:

> that only in wartime do the sexes achieve a normal relationship to each other. The male assumes his dominant heroic role, and the female, playing up to the male, assumes her proper and normal function of being feminine, glamorous and inspiring. With the arrival of peace a decline sets in. The male becomes primarily a meal ticket and the female becomes a sexless frump, transferring her interest from the male to various unproductive intellectual pursuits or to neurotic occupations, such as bridge or politics. Feminine civilization thus goes to pot until a new challenge in the form of wartime psychology restores the balance.

The real intent of such ideology should be obvious from its barbarous, vulgar, fascist essence. The aim of this and other numerous anti-women "theories" is to hamper and curb women's progressive social participation, particularly in the struggle for peace. This has been the alpha and omega of bourgeois ideological attacks upon women since the post-war betrayal of our nation's commitments to its wartime allies.

Such ideology accompanies the developing economic crisis and penalizes especially the Negro women, the working women and the working class generally, but also women on the farms, in the offices and in the professions, who are increasingly entering the struggle to resist the worsening of their economic status.

Not always discerned by the labor-progressive forces, however, is the nature of this ideological attack, which increasingly is masked as attacks on woman's femininity, her womanliness, her pursuit of personal and family happiness. Big capital accelerates its reactionary ideological offensive against the people with forcible opposition to women's social participation for peace and for her pressing economic and social demands.

None of these attacks, however, has been as rabid as the recent "foreign agent" charge falsely leveled by the Department of Justice against the Congress of American Women on the basis of that organization's former affiliation with the Women's International Democratic Federation.

Only the most naive, of course, are startled at the attack against this progressive women's organization, whose policies, domestic and inter-national, were always identified with the progressive camp. The C.A.W. leadership, in its press statement, answered the continuing attack of the Justice Department, which demands "retroactive compliance" with the undemocratic Kellar-McCormack Act, despite the organization's disaffiliation from the W.I.D.F. (under protest). The statement pointed out that this organization has been harassed from its very birth precisely because of its advanced policy stand and activities for peace, child welfare and education, Negro-white unity and equal rights for women. Incumbent on labor-progressives is the expression of full support for the struggles of women against these and other attacks and for the National Bread and Butter Conference of Child Care to be held in Chicago on April 15–16. The call for this conference indicates a broad, united-front sponsorship that includes C.A.W. leaders and demands use of government surpluses and the diversion of war funds to feed the nation's needy children.

Economic Conditions of Women Workers

Any true assessment of women's present status in the United States must begin with an evaluation of the effects of the growing economic crisis upon the working women, farm women, workers' wives, Negro women, women of various national origins, etc. The ruthless Taft-Hartley-employer drive to depress the workers' wage standards and abolish labor's right to strike and bargain collectively, as well as the wholesale ouster of Negro workers from many industries, was presaged by the post-war systemic displacement of women from basic industry. While women constituted 36.1 percent of all workers in 1945, this figure was reduced to 27.6 percent by 1947. Despite this, there still remains a sizable force of 17 and a half million women workers in industry, approximately three million of whom are organized in the trade unions, the vast majority still being unorganized.

The sparse economic data available show that the burdens of the crisis are increasingly being placed on the backs of women workers, who receive unequal wages, are victims of speed-up, and face a sharp challenge to their very right to work. Older women workers are increasingly being penalized in the growing layoffs. Close to 30 percent of the estimated 6 million unemployed are women workers.

Side by side with this reactionary offensive against their living standards, women workers have increasing economic responsibilities. More than half of these women, as revealed in a survey by the Women's Bureau of the U.S. Department of Labor, are economic heads of families. The continued expulsion of women from industry, the growing unemployment of men and youth, as well as the high, monopoly-fixed prices of food and consumer goods generally, are impoverishing the American family and taking a heavy toll on the people's health.

Impoverishment has hit the farm women to an alarming degree. Almost 70 percent of all farm families earned less than $2000 in 1948, when the growing agricultural crisis was only in its first stage.

Women workers still find a large gap between their wages and those of men doing the same work, which the wages of Negro women are particularly depressed below the minimum wage necessary to sustain life.

There are increasing trends toward limited curricula for women students and limited opportunities for women in the professions. Employment trends also show increasing penalization of married women workers who constitute more than half of all working women.

The attempt by employers to foment divisions between men and women workers—to create a "sex antagonism"—is an increasing feature of the offensive to depress the wages of women and the working class in general. Male workers are being told that the dismissal of married women and the "return of women to the kitchen" will lead to an end of unemployment among the male workers. But this whole campaign against "double earning" and for a "return of women to the kitchen" is nothing but a cloak for the reactionary Taft-Hartley offensive against wages, working conditions, and social security benefits, with a view to a wide-scale dumping of workers, male as well as female.

It must be frankly stated that there has been lethargy on the part of progressives in the labor movement in answering and combating this insolent demagogy. It should be pointed out that the German finance capitalists also used this demagogic line prior to the rise of Hitler. By perpetuating the lying slogan that "woman's place is in the home," monopoly capital seeks to conceal the real source of the problems of all workers.

Consequently, this is a question of attacks, not only against the masses of women, but against the working class as a whole. When we deal with the situation of women workers, we do so not only to protect the most exploited section of the working class, but in order to rally labor-progressives and our own Party for work among the masses of women workers, to lead them into the emerging anti-fascist, anti-war coalition.

Trade Unions and Women Workers

There is every evidence that working women's militancy is increasing, as evidenced last year in strikes in such industries as electrical, communications, packinghouse and in strikes of teachers and white-collar workers. Have labor-progressives grasped the significance of the vital need for a trade-union program based on concrete knowledge of the conditions of the woman worker, an understanding of reaction's attacks on her, economically, politically, socially?

Some Left-progressive unionists are beginning to tackle this problem as a decisive one. In New York District No 4 of U.E., splendid initiative was shown by the official establishment of a Women's Committee. Men and women unionists participate jointly to formulate a program and to combat the growing unemployment trends, especially the ouster of married women and their replacement, at lower wages, by young girls from high schools—a trend that affects the wages of all workers. In this union, also, conferences have been held on the problems of the women workers. Similarly, in Illinois, an Armour packinghouse local held a women's conference with the aim of enhancing the participation of Negro and white women workers; as the result of its educational work and struggle, it succeeded in extending the leave for pregnancy from the previous three-month limit to one year.

But these instances are exceptions and not the rule, and it would be incorrect if we failed to state that attitudes of male supremacy among Left-progressives in unions and elsewhere have contributed to the gross lack of awareness of the need to struggle for women's demands in the shops and departments. This bourgeois ideology is reflected in the acceptance of the bourgeois attitude of "normal toleration" of women in industry as a "temporary" phenomenon. This dangerous, tenacious ideology must be fought, on the basis of recognition that the dynamics of capitalist society itself means the tearing of women away from the home into industry as a permanent part of the exploited labor force. Marx and Engels, the founders of scientific socialism, more than one-hundred years ago exposed the pious hypocrisy of the troubadours of capitalism who composed hymns about the "glorious future" of the family relationship under capitalism; they noted the fact, which many progressives too readily forget, that "by the action of modern industry, all family ties among the proletarians are torn asunder [...] The bourgeoisie has torn away from the family its sentimental veil, and has reduced the family relation to a mere money relation."[3]

The absence of a special vehicle to deal with the problems of women workers in the unions has undoubtedly contributed to dealing with these problems, not as a union question, but solely as a woman's question. It is of course, both. But it must be tackled as a special union responsibility, with the Communists and progressives boldly in the forefront. In many instances this approach would improve rank-and-file struggles for wage increases, against speed-up and around other concrete demands, and would also win militant unionists for active participation within the emerging rank-and-file movements. In this connection, it is also necessary to examine the just complaints of many women trade unionists, particularly on a shop level, who are concerned over the trend toward fewer elected women officers, and the relegation of women merely to appointive positions, as well as the unnecessary pattern of "all-male or-

---

3   *Manifesto of the Communist Party.*

ganization" union structure on many levels.

This entire question requires that we take into account also the position of the wives of trade unionists.

Indicative of the growing militancy of workers' wives is the role of miners' wives, hundreds of whom, Negro and white, recently picketed the empty tipples in the mining camps of West Virginia in support of the "no contract, no work" struggle of their fighting husbands, sons and brothers. Similarly, in the longshore trade, during the Local 968 strike in New York, wives of workers, particularly Negro and Italian women, played an outstanding role. Likewise, in Gary and South Chicago, wives of steel-workers issued open letters of support for the miners' struggle at the steel plant gates, collected food, etc.

Reactionary propaganda is not at all loath to exploit the wrong concepts of many workers' wives, who, because of political backwardness stemming from household drudgery, lack of political participation, etc., often adopt the view that it is the union, or the progressive movement, that robs them of their men in relation to their own home responsibilities.

Attention to the organization of wives and working men by labor progressives and Communists therefore becomes an urgent political necessity. And key to avoiding past errors is the enlisting of women themselves, with the support of the men, at the level of their readiness to struggle.

The Equal Rights Amendment

In the context of these developments and attacks upon women's economic and social status, one must also see the recent passage of the Equal Rights Amendment in the U.S. Senate by a 63–19 vote. The original amendment, sponsored by the National Women's Party, proceeding from an equalitarian concept of women's legal status in the U.S., would have wiped out all protective legislation won by women with the assistance of the trade unions over the past decades. Objection to the original amendment by labor-progressives and by our Party led to the formation of a coalition of some 43 organizations, including such groups as the Women's Trade Union League, the U.S. Women's Bureau, the American Association of University Women, C.I.O. and A.F. of L. unions, the National Association of Negro Women, etc.

A proper approach to such legislation today must primarily be based on recognizing that it is projected in the atmosphere of the cold war, carrying with it a mandate for drafting of women into the armed forces, for the war economy. Without such recognition, the present Amendment, which now urges no tampering with previously won protective legislative gains for women workers, might serve as an effective catch-all for many unwary supporters of equal rights for women.

Despite this danger, Left-progressives should not fail to utilize the broad debate already taking place to expose women's actual status in law; some 1,000 legal restrictions still operate at women's expense in numerous states, and minimum-wage legislation does not exist for over 1 million Negro women domestic workers. A demand for legislative hearings and the exposure of the reactionary attacks now prevalent in numerous state legislatures against the legislative gains of women workers are necessary to guarantee that no bill for equal rights for women becomes the law of the land without proper safeguards protecting the special measures meeting the needs of women workers. Perspective of a necessary referendum carrying a 37-state majority necessary to the bill's passage should not obscure the possibility that passage of the legislation in its present form, or minus the protective clause, could serve as a means of bipartisan electoral maneuvers for 1950 and the passage of the Amendment in its original reactionary form.

A Rich Heritage of Struggle

Before 1908 and since, American women have made lasting contributions in the struggle for social progress: against slavery and Negro oppression, for equal rights for women and women's suffrage, against capitalist exploitation, for peace and for Socialism. Special tribute must be paid those heroic women who gave their lives in the struggle for Socialism and freedom: Elsie Smith, Anna Damon, Rose Pastor Stokes, Fanny Sellins, Williana Burroughs and Grace Campbell. In this period of the U.S. monopoly drive to war and world domination, reaction pays unwilling tribute to the role of the Communist women leaders by its deportation delirium. The present-day struggles of progressive and Communist women merge with the traditions and contributions of such great anti-slavery fighters as Harriet Tubman and Sojourner Truth, of such militant women proletarians as the textile workers of 1848, of such women pioneers as Susan B. Anthony and Elizabeth Cady Stanton, of such builders of America's progressive and working-class heritages as

Kate Richards O'Hare, Mother Jones, Ella Reeve Bloor, Anita Whitney and Elizabeth Gurley Flynn.

March 8 was designated International Women's Day by the International Socialist Conference in 1910, upon the initiative of Clara Zetkin, the heroic German Communist leader, who later electrified the world with her brave denunciation of the Nazis in Hitler's Reichstag in 1933. Already in 1907, Lenin demanded that the woman question be specifically mentioned in Socialist programs because of the special problems, needs and demands of toiling women. Present at the 1910 conference as a representative of the Russian Social-Democratic Labor Party, Lenin strongly supported and urged adoption of the resolution inaugurating International Women's Day. Thus did the American-initiated March 8 become International Women's Day.

The opportunist degeneration of the leadership of the Second International inevitably reduced the struggle for the emancipation of women to a paper resolution. Interested only in catching votes, the Socialist parties paid attention to the woman question only during elections.

Lenin and Stalin restored and further developed the revolutionary Marxist position on the woman question. Thus, Stalin declared:

> There has not been a single great movement of the oppressed in history in which working women have not played a part. Working women, who are the most oppressed of all the oppressed, have never stood aloof, and could not stand aloof, from the great march of emancipation.[4]

Lenin and Stalin taught that the position of working women in capitalist society as "the most oppressed of all the oppressed" makes them more than a reserve, makes them a full-fledged part, of the "regular army" of the proletariat. Stalin wrote:

> The female industrial workers and peasants constitute one of the biggest reserves of the working class [...] Whether this female reserve goes with the working class or against it will determine the fate of the proletarian movement [...] The first task of the proletariat and of its vanguard, the Communist Party, therefore, is to wage a resolute struggle to wrest women, the women workers and peasants, from the influence of the bourgeoisie, politically to educate and to organize the women workers and peasants under the banner of the proletariat [...] But working women [...] are something more than a reserve. They may and should become [...] a regular army of the working class

---

4   *Joseph Stalin: A Political Biography,* p. 65.

[...] fighting shoulder to shoulder with the great army of the proletariat [...].[5]

Women Under Socialism

Complete emancipation of women is possible only under Socialism. It was only with the October Socialist Revolution that, for the first time in history, women were fully emancipated and guaranteed their full social equality in every phase of life.

"Women in the U.S.S.R. are accorded equal rights with men in all spheres of economic, state, cultural, social and political life" (New Soviet Constitution, Article 122).

But equal rights in the U.S.S.R. are not just formal legal rights, which, under bourgeois democracy, are curtailed, where not denied in reality by the very nature of capitalist exploitation. In the Soviet Union, full enjoyment of equal rights by women is guaranteed by the very nature of the Socialist society, in which class divisions and human exploitation are abolished. In bourgeois democracies, equal rights for women constitute at best a programmatic demand to be fought for, and constant struggle is necessary to defend even those rights that are enacted into law.

In the U.S.S.R. equal rights articles in the law of the land are but codifications of already existing and guaranteed reality. No wonder Soviet women express such supreme confidence in Socialism and such love for the people. Their respect for other nations, their profound sympathy with the oppressed peoples fighting for national liberation, is based on the firm conviction that their Socialist country is the decisive factor and leader in the struggle for peace.

Marxism-Leninism rejects as fallacious all petty-bourgeois equalitarian notions. Equal rights under Socialism do not mean that women do not have special protection and social care necessitated by their special function (child bearing, etc.) and special needs which do not apply to men.

Comrade Foster's Contribution

The Communist Party of the U.S.A. has many positive achievements to record during the last 30 years in the field of struggle for women's rights and in promoting the participation of women in the struggle against

---

5   Ibid.

war and fascism.

Outstanding was the recent participation of Party women and of the women comrades who are wives of the 12 indicted leaders of our Party in the mass struggle to win the first round in the Foley Square thought-control trial. And in the continuing struggle against the frame-up of our Party leaders we must involve ever larger masses of women.

Under Comrade Foster's initiative and contributions to the deepening of our theoretical understanding of the woman question, a new political appreciation of our tasks is developing in the Party. Party Commissions on Work Among Women are functioning in the larger districts and in smaller ones. International Women's Day will mark a high point in ideological and political mobilization and in organizational steps to intensify our united-front activities among women, particularly around the peace struggle. As a further contribution to that end, a well-rounded theoretical-ideological outline on the position of Marxism-Leninism on the woman question is being prepared.

Comrade Foster called for theoretical mastery of the woman question as vitally necessary to combat the numerous anti-woman prejudices prevalent in our capitalist society, and the "whole system of male superiority ideas which continue to play such an important part in woman's subjugation." An important guide to the Party's work among women are the following words of Comrade Foster:

> The basic purpose of all our theoretical studies is to clarify, deepen and strengthen our practical programs of struggle and work. This is true on the question of women's work, as well as in other branches of our Party's activities. Hence, a sharpening up of our theoretical analysis of, and ideological struggle against, male supremacy, will help our day-to-day work among women [...].

Comrade Foster particularly emphasized the ideological preconditions for effective struggle on this front:

> But such demands and struggles, vital as they may be, are in themselves not enough. They must be reinforced by an energetic struggle against all conceptions of male superiority. But this is just what is lacking.... An ideological attack must be made against the whole system of male superiority ideas which continue to play such an important part in woman's subjugation. And such an ideological campaign must be based on sound theoretical work.[6]

---

6   William Z. Foster, "On Improving the Party's Work Among Women," *Politi-*

Party Tasks

Following Comrade Foster's article in *Political Affairs*, nine Party Conferences on Work Among Women were held with the active participation of district Party leaders. Two major regional schools to train women cadres were held. An all-day conference on Marxism-Leninism and the Woman Question held at the Jefferson School of Social Science last summer was attended by 600 women and men. These developments evidence a thirst for knowledge of the Marxist-Leninist teachings on the woman question.

But it must be frankly stated that it is necessary to combat all and sundry male supremacist ideas still pervading the labor and progressive movements and our Party. The uprooting of this ideology, which emanates from the ruling class and is sustained by centuries of myths pertaining to the "biological inferiority" of women, requires a sustained struggle. Failure to recognize the special social disabilities of women under capitalism is one of the chief manifestations of male supremacy. These special forms of oppression particularly affect the working women, the farm women and the triply oppressed Negro women; but, in varying degrees, they help to determine the inferior status of women in all classes of society.

Progressive and Communist men must become vanguard fighters against male supremacist ideas and for equal rights for women. Too often we observe in the expression and practice of labor-progressive, and even some Communist, men glib talk about women "as allies" but no commensurate effort to combat male supremacy notions which hamper woman's ability to struggle for peace and security. Too many labor-progressive men, not excluding some Communists, resist the full participation of women, avow bourgeois "equalitarian" nations as regards women, tend to avoid full discussion of the woman question and shunt the problem aside with peremptory decisions. What the promotion of a sound theoretical understanding of this question would achieve for our Party is shown by the initial results of the cadre training schools and seminars on the woman question, many of whose students have begun seriously to tackle male supremacist notions in relation to the major tasks of the movement and in relation to their own attitudes.

The manifestation of bourgeois feminism in the progressive women's movement and also in our Party is a direct result of the prevalence of male superiority ideas and shows the need for our women comrades to study the Marxist-Leninist teachings on the woman question. According to bourgeois feminism, woman's oppression stems, not from the capitalist system, but from men. Marxism-Leninism, just as it rejects and combats the petty-bourgeois "equalitarianism" fostered by Social-Democracy, so it has nothing in common with the bourgeois idiocy of "the battle of the sexes" or the irrational Freudian "approach" to the woman question. These false ideologies must be combated by women labor-progressives and in the first place by women Communists. Key participants in the fight against these ideologies, and in the fight to enlist the masses of women for the pro-peace struggle, must be the advanced trade-union women and women Communists on all levels of Party leadership. All Communist women must, as Lenin said, "themselves become part of the mass movement," taking responsibility for the liberation of women.

We must guarantee that women cadres end isolation from the masses of women, by assigning these cadres to tasks of work among women, on a mass and Party basis. The Women's Commissions of the Party must be strengthened. All Party departments and Commissions must deal more consistently with these questions, putting an end to the false concept that work among women represents "second-class citizenship" in our Party. A key responsibility of all Women's Commissions is increased attention and support to the growing movements of youth.

We must gauge our Party's work among women by our effectiveness in giving leadership and guidance to our cadres in mass work, with a view to concentrating among working-class women and building the Party. To this end, further, working-class and Negro women forces need to be promoted in all spheres of Party work and mass activity.

An examination of our work among women is necessary in all Party districts. There is need of Party conferences on the problems of working women and housewives. The good beginnings of examining the long neglected problems of Negro women must become an integral part of all our future work among women. This arises as an imperative task in the light of the militancy and tenacity of Negro women participating in struggles on all fronts.

Experience shows that a major area of our work should and must be in the field of education, where monopoly reaction and the Roman Catholic hierarchy concentrate in a policy in inculcating militarist, racist, pro-fascist ideology in the minds of our children; of victimizing progressive teachers, of conducting witch-hunts, etc. Where good work has been carried on in this sphere, victories have been won, as in the defeat of reactionary legislative measures directed at progressive teachers. In developing struggles to alleviate the frightful conditions of schooling, particularly in Negro, Puerto Rican, Mexican, and other working-class communities, Communist and progressive women have an opportunity for developing an exceedingly broad union front for successful endeavor.

By connecting the struggle against the seemingly little issues of crowded schoolrooms, unsanitary conditions, lack of child care facilities, etc., with the issues of reactionary content of teaching—racism, jingoism, etc.—the political consciousness of the parent masses can be raised to the understanding of the interconnection between the demand for lunch for a hungry child and the demand of the people for economic security; between the campaign for the dismissal of a Negro-hating, anti-Semitic Mae Quinn from the school system and the fight of the people for democratic rights; between the protest against a jingoistic school text and the broad fight of the people for peace.

In keeping with the spirit of International Women's Day, tremendous tasks fall upon our Party. The mobilization of the masses of Americans, together with the enlisting and activation of women cadres, for heightened struggles for peace and for the special needs of oppressed womanhood, is indispensable to the building and strengthening of the anti-fascist, anti-imperialist, anti-war coalition. In working for a stronger peace movement among the women as such, we must draw the masses of women into the impending 1950 election campaign and thereby, on the basis of their experiences in the struggle, help raise their political consciousness to the understanding of the bipartisan demagogy and the hollowness of Truman's tall promises. Large masses of women can thus be brought to a full break with the two-party system of monopoly capital and to adherence to the third-party movement. In the course of this development, with our Party performing its vanguard task, advanced sections among the working-class women will attain the level of Socialist consciousness and will, as recruited Communists, carry on their struggle among the broad masses of women upon the scientific conviction that the final guarantee of peace, bread and freedom, and the full emancipation of subjected woman-kind, will be achieved only in a Socialist America.

For the Unity of Women in the Cause of Peace![1]
1951

Claudia Jones

The growing surge for peace among the women of our country fully confirms the premise contained in the Resolution that *"the fight for peace has a special meaning to the women of the country"* and that *"without their full involvement no peace campaign can be effective."*

Why there is this elemental peace upheaval among American women is of course no mystery. For the first time, on the bodies of their husbands and sons, the women experience the price of attempted world domination by an aggressive ruling class, which only a short time ago boasted of "easy" victories and a "push button war."

In thousands of working class homes, in the last few weeks, the *"notification to next of kin"* has meant that a father, son or husband will never return from the Korean plains—5,000 miles away. Even as the Harrisburg, Pennsylvania, mother of the first quadruple amputee learned, such "slight injuries" are accompanied by callous War Department statements that the soldier's *"morale is excellent."*

Negro mothers and wives are registering alarm, as they become aware that lynching by court martial and wanton shooting of Negro troops in Korea merge with the growth of terrorization of Negro veterans at

---

[1] **Ed. Note:** Originally published in *Political Affairs*, February 1951, pp. 151-168.

home, as witnessed in the brutal police lynching of the Negro veteran, John Derrick.

Life is cheap to the brass hats these days. Recently, the *Daily Worker* carried a story with a Peking dateline, in which the chairman of the Peking Red Cross stated that one-third of the people killed by MacArthur's troops were children, and forty-five percent were women! Children at play, women washing on the river banks, and peasants working in the fields have been the targets of bombing and strafing by the American armed forces whose so-called "police action" was to bring "freedom" to the "unhappy" Korean people!

With the same cold calculation that planned these barbarous atrocities, U.S. imperialism plans to use the sons of American mothers as "blue chips" in their vicious plot of world conquest, fascism, war and death. Over the radio, Gen. Lucius Clay, the protector of Ilse Koch, and Gen. Mark Clark speak bluntly. Thus did Clark declare: *"[...] in the international poker game we're playing today [...] we need more blue chips; blue chips are boys with guns in their hands."*

War Drive Places New Burdens on Women

This threatened militarization of American youth, who, according to Federal Security Administrator Ewing, are to be prepared for a *"lifetime of mobilization"* means not only personal grief for American women, the breaking up of family life for young women and cheating them of the possibility of marriage and motherhood, but the loss of loved ones and increased economic hardships.

On the family-sized farms, the farm women express deep concern over the fate of their sons in the armed forces. Here, in addition to this general worry, the acute labor shortage, due to the loss of their drafted sons, threatens to drive farm families off the land—since hired labor is made impossible by their shrinking incomes.

In industry, women workers have felt the full blows of the growing war economy—the undermining of their already precarious economic positions due to discrimination, to unequal pay rates, lack of opportunity, etc. They face with special impact the threat of wage freezes, rising prices and additional tax withdrawals from their pay envelopes. Speed-up and ever-rising norms, the Truman threat to increase the hours of work, as well as the growing demands for night work, wreak special havoc with the masses of working women, both as workers and as mothers. And the Negro women—faced with intolerable assaults on their rights and living conditions, and with a practical elimination of the few gains secured in industry during the World War II years—are experiencing growing white chauvinist, Jim-Crow obstacles in their efforts to rise above domestic labor which is the lot of millions of Negro women. These harsh economic conditions of Negro and white working women are accompanied by the general male supremacist attitudes prevailing toward all women workers.

But that is not all. Now new economic hardships face the 18 million women workers. Truman's dictatorial National Emergency Decree carries with it a threat to draft women for total war production. Reminiscent of the bestial Nazi attitude toward women, Big Business, in their profit-mad quest for new sources of cheap labor power and resources, seek to emulate the Nazis who likewise drafted "mädchen in uniform" by the millions, reversing their foul slogan that *"woman must be neither comrade nor beloved but only mother,"* and kitchen slave.

These and other problems confronting women in industry make it incumbent on progressives to take the initiative in the fight for the demands of the women workers; to guarantee their integration into the unions; to eliminate the age-old wage differentials and secure equal pay for equal work; and to take special measures to protect the rights of the triply-exploited Negro women workers, as stressed in the main report of Comrade Hall. Side by side with this is the necessity to fight for special social services for women workers, and to wage a struggle for the promotion of women trade unionists to posts of union leadership.

A feature of the growth of fascization in any country, Dimitroff told us, is the cynicism expressed toward the feelings and role of women. A recent Mid-Century White House Conference on the Problems of Youth dared to tell American mothers that their "love" can make children "accept worry about war, put up with poverty and make the best of mediocre schooling."

Women are Speaking out for Peace

But to these and sundry ideological exhortations directed against women's participation in the cause of peace and social progress, in the struggle to ward off attacks on the living standards of their families, and in defense of the democratic and civil rights of the people, American women are daily giving their answer. They reflect the new moods and express the new possibilities for stopping the warmakers. More and more the women are acquiring the consciousness that they will really be to blame if they fail to speak up in defense of their children and their country. That is why they have raised the mass slogans of the camp of peace to end the war in Korea and to bring our boys home.

In the industrial heart of America, a Pittsburgh mother puts an ad in a newspaper simply saying, "Will families of loved ones now trapped in Korea, please call me" and in a single day over 300 mothers responded to this call. Soon, this action is emulated in Akron, Chicago, Detroit, Boston, demanding that Truman bring the boys home. Negro mothers angrily forward letters from their sons in Korea to the N.A.A.C.P. urging speedy intervention against court-martial of their sons who are the scapegoats of MacArthur's military disasters. When in the shops, in the packinghouse, electrical and garment industries, working women form the active core of peace fighters who sent thousands of Christmas greeting cards to Truman with the same demands; when in Eugene, Oregon, 84 Gold Star mothers voice the same demands, then here is confirmation of a widespread peace ferment among the masses of working women.

American women have begun to expose the futility and immorality of the A-bomb as a weapon to solve problems between nations. That is why they are beginning to join their voices with that of their wrathful anti-fascist sisters the world over whose role for peace cannot be over estimated.

American women have begun the embattled cry for peace! And that cry is growing in volume among the innumerable women of the land. This determination to stop war—to impose peace—is growing not only among working class women, Negro and white, but among Quakers, church women, intellectuals, pacifist groups, every national group and organized section of the women masses, young and old.

A Distinct Women's Peace Movement

Comrades! We must now pose the question: How can we most effectively reach the overwhelming majority of women to act for peace? How can we help to convert desire for peace into organization and struggle? How can we help to anchor a women's peace movement, embracing a majority of women, to a working class base which will guarantee it consistency, principle and militancy?

To answer this question, we must pose yet another. Why must there be a distinct women's peace movement? Clearly, it is obvious that no mass peace movement is possible among the Negro people without 51 percent of its population being involved; without its most highly exploited and highly organized sector, the Negro women being organized for peace. No labor peace movement is possible without the millions of women workers decisively represented in the textile, garment, needle, laundry, packinghouse, food and other industries. No working class base can be secured without the organization of seamen's wives, railroad workers' wives, longshore men's wives, wives of steel workers, miners, etc. No movement for peace can be secured unless large masses of national group and farm women are organized for peace, as well as the specially oppressed Mexican American and Puerto Rican women.

Yet, we do not find full agreement on the necessity to organize women, as women, in the peace camp. In numerous pre-Convention discussions, in our National Women's Commission, particularly, we have been involved in discussions about the necessity for such a distinct women's peace movement. We all agreed that this perspective must be fully registered and fought for at our 15th National Convention, since it is no secret that the present level of women's peace activity, which represents a new level in our work among women, has developed with little or no help from male comrades. Indeed, they were often guilty of impeding its development. But in the course of our discussions, we found that full clarity did not exist among our women cadres on the character of such a movement. How did this show itself?

Two tendencies emerged in our discussions. First was the tendency which argued that, since an outstanding weakness of the past was the failure to build united-front movements among working class and Negro women, it was now necessary to limit ourselves to the organization of a working class women's peace movement. Clearly such a tendency is wrong. It fails to understand the full concept of our Party's united-front peace policy which is to create a movement based on the working class in unity with all other peace-loving peoples. It reflects a lack of faith in the working class women themselves who can and will lead all strata of the women in their struggle for peace. This tendency has "Left"-sectarian implications. For to defeat the war makers, it is necessary to unite all sections of the women under the leadership of the working women, as it is necessary to unite its broad allies under the leadership of the working class.

Second was the tendency to see the need of bringing into being a peace movement embracing all women. Such comrades argued that the broad masses of women in our land, because of their oppressed social status in present-day society, because of their role as mothers, as the creators of life, are deeply opposed to war and can be won in their majority to peace. However, in presenting this generally sound point of view, the comrades underestimated the need that such a movement be rooted first of all among working class women, Negro and white. This tendency had certain Right-opportunist implications because there was absent the understanding that the sharp turn to the working class, required in all phases of Party work, applied to the field of work among women as well.

In overcoming these wrong tendencies, after considerable discussion our National Women's Commission correctly stressed the primacy of the working class orientation while recognizing the new opportunities which exist to create a broad women's peace movement among non-working class women in every community, and on all levels. Major attention must be given to organizing the millions of workers' wives in basic industry, the millions of working class housewives in industrial cities, the millions of working class and Negro women who can be won on the peace issue and around the struggle for their burning demands.

Organize Working Women for Peace

But this is still not all that needs to be said on the necessity for a distinct women's peace movement. Our comrades often tell us when we raise this question of the necessity of a working class base for the women's peace movement that working women are already involved in peace activities in their shops. True enough, we discover, as one comrade reported in the splendid panel on Work Among Women, in the New York State Party Convention, that the only peace committee in an upstate electrical plant was organized by women workers—*in the last two weeks.* And this is true of other plants. Working women, who have most sharply felt the effects of the war economy, who face the greatest grief in the contemplated draft of millions of their sons and husbands, of course have risen to spark the fight for peace now finding expression in the shops.

But this does pose a problem, namely, *how can working women participate specifically in the women's peace movement?*

An example of a recent experience in Chicago may be worthwhile as a guide in answering this question. Here, a Women's Committee of the National Labor Conference For Peace was established. This peace committee's role was mainly that of issuing general leaflets which met with little response until they realized that general agitation was not enough; that they had to develop a specific approach to the women, as women. It was then that they issued a leaflet entitled: *Must Babies Die,* which showed the senseless murder of children by the atom bomb and linked the desires of women all over the world—the women of the Soviet Union, China,

France, Africa, Latin America, who joined in the world-wide campaign behind the Stockholm Peace Pledge—who want life for their children, not death. The response was immediate. Over 100 working women responded, mostly from the working class communities, expressing their wish to join peace committees.

Our comrades and other progressive women concluded that this experience is a clue to the organization of working women. It showed them that women can be aroused to action, in their specific role as mothers and wives who want peace, so that their children of today and those yet unborn may grow up to manhood and womanhood. But more than that. They also drew the conclusion that working women who have the double task of working in shops and caring for the home and the family can often better be organized for peace in the communities where they live than in the shops. Those women trade unionists who spark the fight for peace in the shops have a duty and responsibility to tie themselves up with the general women's peace movement, providing that working class leadership so essential to greater stability and militancy of the women's peace movement.

The great potential of this distinct women's peace movement is yet to be fully unleashed and can only be unfolded if women are specifically organized as women.

Our responsibility to our own people, to the masses of women, to the anti-fascist women the world over, is to guarantee that we influence and give leadership to this wide peace sentiment expressed by women, to transform that sentiment into a mighty movement for lasting peace and defense of the needs of the children! Broad united fronts can be developed on the issue of the draft, and against the militarization of the 18-year-olds; on ending the Korean war, and bringing the boys home; on ending the court-martial of Negro troops; on seating the Chinese

Peoples Re public in the U.N. It is also necessary to unmask the war propaganda of the ruling class, in all its forms. There is a grave lack in the peace movement generally to carry through such an exposure.

In this wise, through the creation of a powerful women's peace movement, American women, Negro and white, will take their proper place in the powerful world peace camp with their peace-loving sisters the world over.

Women the World Over Fight for Peace

In over 60 lands, forming a strong sector of the world camp of peace, democracy and Socialism, women are organized in huge federations for peace, security, and defense of their children. Led by the Women's International Democratic Federation, the activities of these millions of peace-loving, anti-fascist women serve to inspire American women to emulate these powerful struggles of their sisters for equality, a happy life for all children and, above all, for a lasting peace.

This new phenomenon—of world-wide identification and sisterhood of women—grew out of the years of boundless suffering by women under fascism and during the anti-fascist war. Women, in the technically advanced countries, suffered outrageous degradation. They learned and experienced the lot of their sisters in the colonial and imperialist oppressed countries. Coupled with this was the uprooting of all bourgeois-democratic relationships involving women, the extermination of whole families and generations of families. It was these and other costly experiences that gave rise to the new determination of women throughout the world that never again would they allow the use of their sons for the imperialist slaughter of other nations and peoples.

Impelling these developments is the leadership of the world camp of peace, democracy and Socialism by a workers' state—the Socialist Soviet Union, which has exemplified in life its concern for the well-being and full equality of women and full protection of children in all spheres. The world-shaking ex-ample of free Soviet womanhood, the new freedoms achieved by the liberated woman in the lands of the European Democracies who move toward Socialism, the historic strides—as a result of the Chinese People's Revolution—in the elimination of the feudal bondage formerly experienced by millions of downtrodden women of China—all are decisive contributing factors explaining why there now exists a powerful international anti-fascist, anti-imperialist women's movement.

American women bear a heavy responsibility to the millions of our anti-fascist sisters in the world camp of peace, precisely because the threat to world peace stems from the imperialists of our land. The repeated appeals to American women from the embattled mothers of Greece, Franco Spain and the Marshall-Plan-saddled countries are staunch reminders of the responsibilities women in the United States bear to the world struggle for peace and anti-fascism.

The pro-fascist Department of Justice attacks last year against the international fraternization of women should lead us to conclude that we face a great responsibility, in the sphere of work among women, to the high principles of proletarian internationalism. In great measure, our meeting of that responsibility depends on the support given by labor-progressives, led by our vanguard party, the Communist Party, to the emerging women's peace movement. Through such support, the struggle for the equality of women will merge with the general class struggle of the working class which understands and defends the needs and demands of the masses of women. Support to the peace struggles of women in our country will thereby also help to bring in line with world developments, based on American experience, a new advance in women's status in our country.

A Women's Peace Center

Comrade Hall properly stressed the necessity for our Party to help nurture, support and encourage the development of such a movement. Already existing in our land is a progressive peace center of women which should be seen in relationship to the whole perspective of winning and organizing women for peace. The American Women for Peace, represents the center of coalescing women's peace sentiment, composed of broad peace forces who have identified themselves with a specific women's peace movement. Though not all-inclusive of the peace forces among women, this center is already playing a signal role in the country. It has led three major actions for peace—on the anniversary of Hiroshima, on U.N. Founding Day, and on November 28, when Truman brazenly announced he was considering use of the A-bomb in Korea and Manchuria. On that day, over 2,500 women, on 36 hours notice, appeared before the U.N. demanding the outlawing of the A-bomb and the ending of the inhuman Korean adventure. Here, the splendid initiative and leadership of this women's peace center was clearly demonstrated.

One should note that this activity has not gone unnoticed by the world camp of peace. The returned women delegates to the World Peace Congress tell audiences everywhere they speak, that the first toast by Soviet Peace Chairman Tikhonov, given on their visit to the land of Socialism, was to the delegation of women who went to the U.N. on its founding day, *"who got there before the men did."* The regularly issued News-Brief of the Women's International Democratic Federation reported the November 28 women's peace action with the observation that this "was the first news to reach them" of the world-wide outraged protest of women against Truman's madness. In quite a different vein, Eleanor Roosevelt was forced to state demagogically, despite her Red-baiting adjectives, that the November 28 U.N. women's delegation *"spoke the yearning in the hearts of every woman in the land for peace."*

To expand the unity of women for peace, we must reject concepts which deny the need for a distinct women's peace center on the grounds that we need a "broader movement and broader forces." These arguments come especially from those who stand on the sidelines, criticizing what exists under the guise that the peace center is not yet all-inclusive, while doing nothing to reach those "broader forces." On the other hand is the argument that the peace center is not "militant enough," not sufficiently advanced. This argument reflects a failure to understand that the level of the present activity of this peace center, which is not anti-imperialist or even anti-fascist but an expression of the general peace strivings of women, is in keeping with their present level of experience. It will reach a higher level of understanding and militancy as it expands its activity and especially as it organizes peace committees below, of women from the decisive working class strata. We cannot substitute our own desires for militancy for a broad peace movement, as some of our comrades and advanced progressives sometimes seek to do artificially. If we do that we will be militant by ourselves.

Precisely because this women's peace center views its task not only as one of serving as a center of women's peace activities on a minimum united-front basis, but also for stimulating and organizing women's peace committees on a community level, it merits the wholehearted support of Communist and progressive women. Issuance of a splendid regular monthly Bulletin by A.W.P., *The Peacemaker*, for $1 a year is a splendid vehicle for exchange of experiences of women in the fight for peace. It can serve as an organ which links the woman's movement to other developments and trends in the broad labor and people's peace movement. Progressive women everywhere should subscribe to this organ as a major means of assisting its work.

In addition, Communist and progressive women everywhere must give leadership to women in their communities, and their organizations on such issues as the terror creating atomic air raid drills, the inadequate school appropriations, the skyrocketing prices, higher taxes, etc., and other such issues which affect the women and their families. These issues in many instances, can serve as the starting point for involving women in broader peace activities.

Negro Women Fight for Peace

In our efforts to help build a peace movement of women, we must once and for all overcome the gap between the influence of the triply oppressed Negro women, expressed in their own mass organizations and in the Negro people's movement generally, and their role in the organized peace movement. We must multiply a thousand fold the leadership of Negro women in the fight for peace. In examining our work in the building of peace committees, our greatest weakness, second only to that of building women's peace committees in working class areas, is the failure to establish peace committees among Negro women. Can it be claimed that Negro women feel less strongly about peace than do other sections of women? The facts contradict this absurdity. As the wife of William McGee[2] played an outstanding role in the fight against the rising terror and intensified oppression of Negro citizens at home, so it was the wife of Lt. Leon Gilbert whose initiative broke the case of her court-martialed officer husband.

The outstanding peace heroines of the Stockholm Peace Petition campaign were Negro women—Molly Lucas of Illinois and Jackie Clack of California—who were sent as delegates to the Warsaw Peace Congress and had the opportunity to visit the U.S.S.R. In Harlem, Bedford-Stuyvesant, Boston's South End, Philadelphia's 4th Ward, and similar areas, thousands of signatures of Negro mothers and wives

---

2   Ed. Note: William McGee (1916-1951) was a Black man falsely convicted by an all-white jury, and executed by the state of Mississippi. His court case was followed worldwide by progressive campaigners and was seen as representative of the many miscarriages of justice and "legal lynchings" that were carried out by Jim Crow courtrooms.

were affixed to the world-wide petition which called for outlawing as war criminals the atomaniacs who first use the bomb. In all peace delegations of women, almost one-third were Negro women. Why then is there no commensurate movement of Negro women for peace?

Contributing to this state of affairs no doubt was the white chauvinist hesitation to raise the Negro question in the broad labor and people's peace movement, particularly in the context of America's imperialist aggression against the colored peoples of Asia. Additional reasons may be found in the continued efforts of Negro reformists and bourgeois nationalists to sell the Negro people the idea that this is "their war"; in the whipping-up of false jingoistic moods of contempt even among Negro troops for their Korean brothers; and in reaction's veiled flattery of Negro troops in the early stages of the war—to cover what we now know was tipping their hats to the expendability of Negro troops based on chauvinist contempt for the lives and welfare of Negro soldiers.

Now, more than ever, the Negro people understand the full significance of U.S. military aggression in Korea. They see in the bloody massacre of the people of Korea an extension of the foul white supremacy Oppression and contempt for the Negro people to the colored people of all of Asia. It is therefore possible to organize the broadest type of peace activities among the Negro people, and particularly among Negro women. This is necessary in the self-interest of the Negro people. And the merger of this anti-imperialist current with the broader labor, people's, women's and youth peace movements, will greatly strengthen the peace camp as a whole.

In the growing anger of Negro mothers against military lynching by court-martial, in the embittered recognition of Negro mothers and wives that their fighting husbands and sons are dying for a cause that is not their own lies the key to arouse and organize their sentiment for peace. In such activity, a new understanding will arise; they will begin not only to question, as they are already doing, why their sons are expendable, but why it is necessary to fight at all in Korea—why it is necessary to fight in any far-off lands.

A hallmark of the recognition by the American bourgeoisie of the special role women play in the Negro liberation movement is their "courtship" of Negro women. But this "courtship" is to be compared to the white supremacist who prates his superiority, but sneaks into the homes of Negro women, invading their privacy, impugning their dignity and perpetuating their social degradation in our society. Thus did Truman,

Acheson and Dubinsky's Pauline Newman attend the recent national convention of the prominent National Council of Negro Women, in order to align this Negro women's organization with the Truman war program. The bourgeois chauvinist contempt of Negro women is so great that even the U.N. appointment of an Edith Sampson is not on the basis of leadership ability of Negro women but admittedly "to counter Russian propaganda."

To fully expose the false and lying purpose of this imperialist courtship, rejected by millions of Negro women, means a sharp unequivocal struggle against the special forms of white chauvinism directed against Negro women.

There is widespread evidence, as shown in experience in the women's peace and other mass movements, also reflected in our Party, that the struggle against the special forms of white chauvinism toward Negro women is not yet recognized as a struggle in the basic self-interest of white women. Indeed this was glaringly evidenced in the shameful white chauvinist remarks of an invited woman comrade to the splendid Women's Panel of the New York State Party convention, who expressed herself to the effect that the Negro women on her P.T.A. board were *"mealy mouthed."* Imagine! Failure of a Negro woman to actively participate in the activity of the P.T.A. is blamed on her, and not on the crude white chauvinist atmosphere which permeates most of these organizations.

The stifling white chauvinist atmosphere within these organizations stems largely from their overwhelmingly petty-bourgeois composition. It is likewise reflected in the failure to conduct struggles for the social needs of Negro women and their children against dilapidated pre-Civil War schools, against segregation within the school system, against the practice of organizing in Negro, Puerto Rican, and Mexican communities classes for the "retarded," thus deliberately perpetuating the discriminatory status in the schooling of these children. To state that Negro women, even of petty-bourgeois composition, do not themselves conduct such struggles is tainted with white chauvinism. It avoids the prime responsibility of white women to lead in the fight against these appalling conditions.

We can accelerate the militancy of Negro women to the degree with which we demonstrate that the economic, political and social demands of Negro women are not just ordinary demands, but special demands, flowing from special discrimination facing Negro women as women, as workers and as Negroes. It means first, to unfold the struggle for jobs, to organize the unorganized Negro women workers in hundreds of open-shop factories and to win these job campaigns. It means overcoming our failure to organize the domestic workers who recently won for the first time the begrudging official recognition of the status of "workers" in the social security regulation changes. It means more than a pious sympathy for Rosa Lee Ingram, imprisoned for over 3 years, and a revival of the campaign for her speedy release. It means that we must not allow on the Lower East Side a Settlement House to close because bourgeois Jewish nationalists say: "It was meant for Jewish children and now there are too many Puerto Ricans and Negroes." Yes, and it means that a struggle for social equality for Negro women must be boldly fought for in every sphere of relations between men and women so that the open door of Party membership doesn't become a revolving door because of our failure to conduct this struggle.

Women's Special Issues and Demands

Comrades, I have singled out three main questions in this sub-report flowing out of the splendid report of Comrade Hall, namely: 1) the necessity to develop, strengthen and build a distinct women's peace movement; 2) the rooting of that movement among working women and the wives of workers; and 3) the special necessity to bring the fight for peace to the Negro women.

But we all know that analysis and experiences in struggle, sound though these may be, are not enough. The key to nurture, expand and coalesce these peace strivings of women means the raising of special demands, of special issues and the development of special forms of organization. We have much to learn from the rich experiences of the international anti-fascist women's movement, especially from France and Italy, as well as Argentina and Africa, where a feature of these movements is the distinct peace struggle of women linked with defense of the needs of children.

One of the key issues which grips the heart of every mother and fills her children's hearts with terror are the newly introduced atomic air-raid drills now taking place in the nation's schools. But can it be said that progressive women have grasped the possibilities for peace struggle inherent in the widely expressed new sentiment which shows that women and particularly mothers are not accepting this program? Newspaper editorials, the statements of public figures as well as our own knowledge from ties with the people, shows in city after city that despite whipping up of anti-Soviet hysteria, volunteers are not forthcoming and there has not been mass identification with the civilian defense apparatus. No doubt what contributes to this is that millions of women and mothers cannot see security from war in a civilian defense set-up that is nationally headed by the former Governor Caldwell—a Dixiecrat from Florida, and in New York, by the anti-Semite Gen. Lucius Clay, and by similar characters in other states.

We can neither encourage false security in a program which is based on the false idea of the inevitability of war, nor ignore the sentiments which impel response and concern, even though passive, by millions to this program. We are duty bound, however, to expose the falsity of this program and the instigators of this program, the very ones who threaten the use of the atomic bomb.

Let us boldly place the question right side up. Let us tell mothers who are worried about atomic warfare that the only defense—even with shelters, drills and war preparations—is to ban the atomic bomb. In many cities children die in congested streets, and mothers have to build living islands of safety with their bodies before a traffic light is installed. Shall we say nothing about such a city spending thousands of dollars on a shelter—which in New York City costs $47,000? Shall we be silent about the use of money for these shelters being built in swanky communities while working class children and Negro children cower in dank pre-Civil War school rooms which need to be torn down?

The cost of a single battleship could provide 325 family-sized dwelling units. Shall this money be used for a false national emergency in which 70 billions are being spent for bombs or shall the money be spent for housing projects and homes?

In addition to this vital issue is the issue of high prices, another weakness of the women's movement. Yet experience shows that this issue of high prices is one of the most powerful and effective issues around which women will respond; and in seeing the connection between their immediate demands and the struggle for peace, they will also see a necessity for a change in the political administration that denies to them and their families these basic needs.

Generally on the question of the defense of the needs of children there is need for a new appreciation of the prime necessity of strengthening our support to progressive leadership in the parent-teacher field. In numerous states, it has been the consistent activity of progressive and Communist mothers, whose leadership, together with teachers, has helped to counter the racist witch hunts, has fought disastrous pro-fascist legislation which threatens to penalize progressive teachers, and who have generally challenged the drive to fascize the minds of our children. The fiasco of the Freedom Scroll campaign in Los Angeles and San Francisco, opposed by the parent-teacher movement, is an example of the readiness of women to struggle on these issues. Every city budget hearing, where the axe is being put to school needs, finds women present—aroused and fighting in defense of their children's needs. These and other examples should point up to labor-progressives and our Party the wealth of mass issues to rally women and mothers on; and to the possibilities in struggle to raise their political consciousness on the necessity of the struggle for peace.

Comrades, the politics of the women's movement today is not at all simple but complicated. All that Comrade Hall said relative to skill in tactics is being raised as our women comrades, together with non-Party women peace fighters, grapple with these and other problems. In New England the organization, Minute Women for Peace, is under fierce attack. The bourgeoisie, the state and city officials of New England—the cradle of American liberty—are afraid because the present-day sisters of Molly Pitcher, of Deborah Gannett, of the early textile women strikers for the 10-hour-day are fighting for peace, to preserve liberty. To defeat these and other attacks means to guarantee support to the struggle of these women peace fighters. Involved here is the right of fraternal association with our sisters from other lands which received a severe blow at the hands of the warmongers in the recent period. Winning this struggle also means defending the principle of the right of Communist women to work among, and earn leadership among the masses of women, in order to help dissolve the foul tissue of lies about women's capability and leadership in women's struggle for peace and progress.

Our Party's Work Among Women

To help transform women's peace sentiment into a mighty organized movement for peace, security, equality and defense of children, means we must change our Party's methods of work and approaches to our own women cadre.

In his report, Comrade Hall stated that:

> the worst symptom of male superiority tendencies in our ranks is the speed with which we released the bulk of our leading women comrades after World War II—and our slowness to correct this error. The new level of work achieved by our women comrades, and the new currents stirring among the masses of women, must be reflected in our Party's new level of understanding of the woman's question, This goes for our entire leadership and membership.

What is necessary to achieve this *"new level of understanding"* in work among women? It means, first of all, recognizing and applying the Leninist concept that Communist women must *"themselves be part of the mass movement of women."* It means the virtual release of dozens and dozens of our women comrades for work among women for peace and to struggle for women's special demands.

In many Party sections a consciousness exists that in order to make it possible for women to participate generally in Party activities, the obstacles to women's full participation must be recognized. Party cadres here understand that because under capitalism, care of children is more than often the sole responsibility of women, and not viewed as a social responsibility, as is the case under Socialism, it is necessary to provide for baby sitters to help release women for general Party work. But examination shows that this practice, limited because of its costliness, is not widespread. Nor is the same approach taken to release Party women cadre for work among the masses of women. Coupled with this a general underestimation of work among women is expressed in the practice of taking practically all of our women comrades out of their natural habitat thus robbing them of their mass contacts in P.T.A.'s and women's organizations while they function as general Party actives.

Then there is the general male supremacist approach which relegates only certain phases of responsibility to women on the assumption that women aren't ready for top leadership responsibilities on a policy-making level. The fact that in the basic units of our Party a great deal of leadership is exercised by our women cadres refutes this assertion. But what is required here is the elevation of women to policy-making bodies of the Party organization.

There are literally dozens of women in every Party section who, viewing such practices, ask: How can women function fully in the Party—

women with families and children, whose problems cannot be fully solved under capitalism? Of course women can and do function as general Party activists and that is all to the good, but they function as general Party activists, and not among the masses of women. The splendid results shown in not a few communities where women were released for work among women, shows how fully one-half of the Party's effectiveness could be strengthened if our Party leadership on all levels overcomes this general under-estimation of work among women.

Combating Male "Supremacy"

Last summer, when Party reorganization was a prime concern, we learned how costly such attitudes could be. They led to liquidationist trends in our Party expressed in the automatic dropping of women comrades. Male-supremacist attitudes ranged from proposals to pull our women comrades out of mass peace work and work among women generally, to ideas that true security means that women should "protect the kids" by pulling out of Party activity. Here was a case of the intensification of bourgeois feminist notions of what true security is and intensification likewise of male supremacist ideas that "women's place is in the home." When some women resisted, some Party forces even held that women felt the tension more than others even going so far as to hold up as "proof" one woman who had a change of life which is the usual and normal biological manifestation when a woman reaches a certain age!

But true security for the family, including families of Party members, comes in the first place from participation of both male and female members of the family in activity for peace and social progress. True security for the Communist family means not liquidation of women's work but expanding that work on the basis of recognizing that the activization of women generally confounds those who desire to keep one-half of the population in passive acceptance of the false ideas of the inevitability of war and fascism.

Overcoming these male supremacist notions means to recognize moreover that our Party, as distinct from those who hold petty-bourgeois equalitarian notions, fights for the true equality of women. What does this mean? It means fighting for the right of women to enjoy every right and privilege enjoyed by men. Many shout equality in general, but in practice show lack of understanding of the special aspects of equality. The petty bourgeois equalitarian denies the special problems and needs of women. True recognition of the special aspects of equality for women means fighting to squeeze out every concession right here under capitalism relative to fighting women's numerous disabilities and inequalities in the home, on the job, in the community. It means above all fighting for the economic equality of women, because her economic dependence on men in our society, her exclusion from production, makes for a double exploitation of women (and triply so for Negro women) in present-day society. It means support to her special demands, for child-care centers, health centers, etc. It means elevation of women to leadership on all Party levels. It means also taking into account biological differences which contribute to women's special problems. Greater education on what is meant by equality is also needed, with special emphasis, directed as Lenin said, to the men in our Party who should be more self-critical of these weaknesses, and who must overcome their patronizing attitudes to women.

Our pre-Convention discussion raised anew the question of the struggle against many male supremacist manifestations which Comrade Foster over two years ago called upon our entire Party to overcome in ideological struggle. We must register that Foster's contribution made for a decisive turn in our approach to the woman question throughout our Party, as particularly reflected in all major reports to this convention, and in the stress being placed by our Party leaderships in many districts. But there is no need to be complacent on this question since we must use this new awareness to unfold an even greater ideological understanding that there is a Marxist Leninist approach to the woman question. This is not just the responsibility of the National Women's Commission which is already overburdened, and needs assistance on a national level, which needs establishment on a permanent basis of State Party Commissions on work among women, to serve as powerful arms of Party leadership on state levels in work among women, but it requires the conduct of such an ideological campaign by our entire Party.

For Ideological Clarity on Work Among Women

I propose that this Convention instruct our incoming leadership and National Educational Department to launch such a campaign starting on International Women's Day, March 8, 1951. I.W.D. should be the occasion for widespread tribute to the role and potentialities of the masses of women, and to inculcate an understanding of the Marxist-Leninist approach to women in society, as a duty and responsibility of all Communist men and women. One such contribution to this end is the forthcoming volume on the woman question (a collection of the writings of Marx, Engels, Lenin and Stalin) which will be published by International Publishers in January, and which should receive wide circulation and study.

Proper use of the Women's Page of *The Worker*, under the leadership of Peggy Dennis, now widely read; the organization of friends and readers of *The Worker* to make this page the vehicle of exchange of experiences in the peace and general women's movement, can make this page the avenue to increasing the circulation of the press among the masses of women, particularly among Negro and working class women.

The Draft Resolution's failure to deal adequately with the woman question, overcome now with Comrade Hall's report, consists in the fact that it failed not only to deal adequately with women's role—but with her oppression—the crux of the question. It is true that the widespread and justifiable criticism by many of our women comrades of the Resolution's weakness was due to their failure to find a corresponding estimate of work among women on all Party levels. They saw therefore the struggle for women's equality solely as an *inner Party matter*, isolated, as too many of them are from the broad ferment of women for peace. Where women, despite obstacles, plunged ahead, and did not fall into the "battle of the sexes" bourgeois-feminist moods, there recognition of women's full role and contribution to the fight for peace was swiftest. This should point up a great fact: namely, that it is the movement of the women themselves for peace that has forced a new awareness upon our Party and labor-progressive forces everywhere today. A real tribute for this approach goes to Comrade Foster who told us that women must fight for their own liberation, and to women Communist anti-fascist leaders in the international women's movement.

The attention and agreement of the entire Party organization must be won to the solution of, and collective application to these problems. Overcoming of these weaknesses will release the collective talents of our wonderful women comrades to work, write, sing and fight for women's liberation; and they will want to do it not as second-class citizens but as contributors to Party policy and mass work in our clubs and groups.

Promotion of Women Cadres

It is time our Party recognize the precious capital it has in its women cadres. Important indications of an improved attitude in the Party toward the promotion of women in leadership are seen in many parts of the country. We have the advancement to the State Committee at the recent New York Party Convention of such comrades as Lil Gates, Johnnie Lumpkin and Mercedes Arroya; the splendid leadership of such women comrades as Vickie Lawrence and Anne Garfield in work among women in New York and New England; the recent elevation of Comrade Mollie Lieber West to the post of Illinois organizational secretary; of Grace Tillman to a similar position in Indiana and of Comrade Vi to a leading post in a Southern Party district. We have comrades like Rose Gaulden in the leadership in Philadelphia's 4th Ward, of Dorothy Healy and Bernadette Doyle in key positions in California, of Betty Gannett as our National Education Director, of women Communist veterans like Dora Lipshitz and Rose Baron, and that of Martha Stone as District Organizer of New Jersey. We also have emerging Negro women leaders like Mary Adams, the splendid young Party women cadre like Jeanie Griffith and Judy; the inspiring role of the foremost woman leader of our Party, Elizabeth Gurley Flynn, and of the great women veterans like Mother Bloor and Anita Whitney. There are other women cadres too numerous to mention.

Inspired and steeled by the powerful science of Marxism-Leninism, which holds the key to the ultimate liberation of women in a Socialist society, where the basis of women's exploitation is eliminated, exploitation of man by man abolished, and the true equality of the sexes achieved, let us resolve at this 15th National Convention of our Party to honor the Jane Higginses whose daily work is a measure of their desire to master Marxist-Leninist theory, to participate in winning a glorious future.

In this struggle, Communist women, by their leadership among the masses of women, and learning from them to fight for their demands, will fuse the women's peace movement under the leadership of the working class, and will thereby help to change the relationship of forces in our land in such a way as to make for a new anti-fascist, anti-imperialist people's coalition, advancing through this struggle to Socialism.

The Struggle for Peace in the United States[1]
1952

Claudia Jones

President Truman in his capacity as chief political servitor of U.S. imperialism, once again proposed, in his recent State of the Union Message to Congress, a criminal crusade of force and violence against the vast majority of the human race. Truman, though prating about peace, glorified Wall Street's aggressive expansionism which is now flagrantly directed against the colored peoples of Asia and Africa, and proposed an unrestrained armaments race.

Mr. Truman cynically boasted of the colossal size of U.S. imperialism's armed strength, and its pile of A-bombs. By way of perspective for peace, he urged even more intensive arming to be accompanied by further cuts in consumer goods output and in real wages. While he lectured the people about the need for "sacrifice," in a year marked by the largest total profits in the history of American capitalism, he proposed an additional five billions in new taxes.

Truman used hundreds of words in an effort to justify further burdens upon the people, but not a mumbling word did he voice about the terrible repression of civil rights in our country, the political persecution, led by his Administration, of Communist and other working-class leaders. The genocidal oppression of the Negro people, as highlighted

---

1   **Ed. Note:** Originally published in *Political Affairs*, vol. 31, no. 2, February 1952, pp. 1-20.

just before his Message by the killing of Mr. and Mrs. Harry T. Moore, was ignored, and not a phrase fell from his lips about F.E.P.C., or anti-lynching and anti-poll tax measures. Dropped was all talk of the repeal of the Taft Hartley Law, but instead he indulged in a concern for a "fair" version of that slave statute.

Nor could the farming masses derive any satisfaction from the Truman message. A recent Federal report signed by James Patton, President of the National Farmers Union, indicated that two million farmers (in a total of 5-6 million farms) will be forced off the land and into industry to meet the "defense" requirements. When one adds the already heavy drainage of farmers' sons for the armed forces, it is clear that further impoverishment awaits the already greatly harassed lower-income farmers.

Of course, Truman's saber-rattling Message had its "peace-loving" interludes, confirming the accumulating peace sentiment in our country, to which hats must be tipped in accordance with the demands of good campaign strategy. Thus, Truman declared: "[...] day in and day out we see a long procession of timid and fearful men who wring their hands and cry out that we have lost the way—that we don't know what we are doing—that we are bound to fail. Some say that we should give up the struggle for peace and others say we should have a war and get it over with." Mr. Truman "struggles for peace" by putting aside a total of eleven percent of his budget to meet all the needs of all social services!

In his pose as "savior" of the "American way of life," Truman invokes the divine right to impose war's "blessings" on the Korean people and on the rising national-liberation movements of the colonial and dependent countries. Moreover, Truman seeks to convince the American people of the "necessity" to rally behind Wall Street on the basis of a "peril" which he dares term "internal aggression." But Truman perpetrates a gigantic and vicious hoax when he asserts that our nation is in "peril" because the Chinese people do not want Chiang Kai-shek, and the Korean people do not want Syngman Rhee; because the peoples of Egypt and Iran want to control their own natural resources, and because the peoples of Indo-China, Burma, Spain, and Greece want a free, democratic existence. The Truman war program, unless routed, dooms our nation to endless war in which the rich become richer and the poor poorer; it consigns the nation's youth to death for the glory of Wall Street profiteers. The Truman perspective is that of looting the national wealth, of crushing the national aspirations of the freedom-seeking peoples, of extending the Korean adventure into a World War. Stripped of its demagogy, Truman's Message confirmed our Party's estimate that the war danger has heightened, albeit its defensive tone reflects the growing counter-struggle for peace of the masses of workers and the people generally. It likewise reflected growing contradictions of an inter-imperialist character as well as within the US. bi-partisan war coalition, and in effect acknowledged the decisive and ever-increasing strength of the world camp of peace, democracy and Socialism.

The utter futility of the 20-month war in Korea and Ridgway's seven-month stalling of the truce talks have increased the sharp uneasiness of the American people, with whom the Korean war was never popular, and who have long seen it as a threat to world peace.

The startling significance of the Truman-Churchill "secret agreements" to A-bomb Manchuria and to take the war to China, to "save" South-East Asia from its own peoples with the help of hired Chiang mercenaries, armed with American weapons, must be viewed in the light of Truman's fundamental adherence to the criminal bi-partisan war policy, ruinous to our nation and to all humanity. And it is in this light that we must view the current Senate hearings for ratification of the so-called Japanese Peace Treaty signed without the consent of the major Asian powers and without the Soviet Union, the Dulles call for "hardening" of US. policy to "overthrow" the Chinese People's Republic, and the new wave of incendiary war talk.

Setbacks for Wall Street in the U.N. Assembly

The recently concluded Paris U.N. Assembly meeting graphically revealed the real reason for the Truman warning to his NATO allies against "faltering" since the road is "long and hard." For there the exceedingly shaky nature of the coalition forming the U.S. imperialist bloc in the U.N. became clear. It was evident that the satellite delegates could not be held securely by the U.S. imperialist leash of economic sanctions.

Wall Street dollars could not eliminate the justified fear that these representatives have of their impoverished and insulted peoples. Those peoples of Western Europe, Latin America, Africa, Australia, Asia, and the Near and Middle East do not want any part of a war on China. This is shown by the extreme difficulty the U.S. had in forcing a U.N. vote denouncing the Soviet Union for "violating" its 1945 treaty with the Chiang regime, on the "theory" that it is "Soviet aggression" for the Chinese people to sweep out the butcher-regime of Chiang Kai-shek and to inaugurate a self-determined, independent, and democratic People's Republic.

It is in this light that the now tempered bull-dog bark of Churchill is to be understood in his speech to Commons, following his U.S. tour. Nor was this the only moral defeat suffered by the U.S. imperialist bloc at the Assembly meeting. There was, too, the vote on U.N. admission of Greece from which the entire Latin American bloc initially abstained; and not to be forgotten is the significant presentation of the C.R.C. petition, "We Charge Genocide," by William Patterson, precisely at a time when the Wall Street delegation was boasting of "human rights" and at a moment when the eyes of the world were on Florida, scene of the genocide bombing of Mr. and Mrs. Harry T. Moore.

New Moods for Peace

Over a year ago, Gus Hall, in his main Report to the 15th National Convention of the Communist Party, said, truly and profoundly:

> The clearer the war danger becomes, the more people move in defense of peace. This new upsurge is based on a new appreciation of the war danger, on a growing realization that the present course of the bi-partisans has led to a dead end. It is based on a growing confidence that peace can be won. The new turn of events in Korea packed a double wallop because millions of Americans were never enthusiastic about this reckless adventure and were never sold on the idea that this was a war for which they should willingly make sacrifices. [...] We must be confident that we are going to win the working class as a class, the Negro people as a people. And that the poor farmers, church groups, and large sections of the middle class are going to participate in the organized peace movement. A powerful American peace front is clearly emerging from these developments. This peace front will be based on the working class, the Negro people, poor and middle farmers, and yes, sections of the capitalist class. This is especially true of the capitalist elements who see their imperialist aims best fulfilled on the "continent" and those closely tied to agriculture.[2]

The subsequent months have vindicated Comrade Hall's analysis. There has been and there is a maturing peace sentiment among the American people, heightened during the U.S. imperialist deliberately stalled Korean truce talks. A striving is evident amongst broader and broader masses for an over-all negotiated settlement of all outstanding

---

2   *Peace Can Be Won!*, by Gus Hall, New Century Publishers, 1951, p. 24.

differences among nations. Even the Gallup Poll reported seventy per cent of the American people desired a Truman-Stalin meeting devoted to resolving U.S.-U.S.S.R. differences, The growing peace sentiment stems not only from new sections of the population as a whole, but primarily from new sections of the working class and Negro people. More and more the inequality of "sacrifice" and the genocidal policy towards the colored peoples abroad and at home serve to expose the sickening hypocrisy in the Truman bi-partisan foreign policy. These peace moods are reflected not only in growing queries and doubts, but in an insistent note that our country take a new path—that it reverse its present bi-partisan war policy for a path of negotiation of outstanding differences between nations and for a Big Five Power Peace Pact. This note has a real grassroots quality and is being sounded more and more frequently and openly by mothers, wives, veterans, youth, and G.I.'s themselves. Despite continued and sharpened governmental harassment of the advanced defenders of peace, a "second look" is being taken as increasing masses weigh the real alternative to the bi-partisan dead-end—the principle of negotiation between nations, which, premised on the concept of peaceful co-existence of states with different social systems, can lead to the conclusion of a Five-Power Peace Pact.

These masses, faced by declining real wages and mounting unemployment, demonstrate a growing awareness that it is the war economy which is responsible for this suffering and are moving to challenge more boldly the monstrous bi-partisan "alternative" of an "all-out war" to "get it over with quick" or a huge armaments race and "more Koreas."

The development of these peace sentiments is not the result of a sudden awakening but rather stems from a process of long duration. Among the many forces stimulating the growth of these desires have been the 110,000 reported U.S. battle casualties, the cynical seven-month long delay in the truce talks, the open alliance of the U.S. rulers with Japanese and Nazi militarists and fascists, and the immense rise of the worldwide peace struggle exemplified by the liberation efforts in Asia, the Near East and Africa, the mounting hatred of U.S. imperialism throughout Europe, and the signing of the demand for a Five-Power Peace Pact by over six hundred millions of world humanity.

What is taking place is the *beginning* of a basic re-evaluation of the suicidal anti-Soviet premise of the Truman bi-partisan policy. And this applies to large masses who have not yet broken with monopoly capital's two-party system and are still attracted by the "peace" demagogy of one or another bi-partisan spokesman.

While trade-union leaders in ever increasing numbers cry out for an end to the Korean war and the anti-imperialist sentiments of the Negro people reach an all-time high level; while Truman's "holy war" propaganda is delivered a blow by the defeat of his proposal to appoint General Mark Clark as Ambassador to the Vatican; while the whole State Department effort to make peace "subversive" suffers a blow in the great victory of the acquittal of Dr. Du Bois and his associates of the Peace Information Center—at such a time Truman still waves the threat of atom-bomb superiority and projects new proposals for extending hostilities.

And Truman does not repudiate the hideous statement of his field commander in Korea, Gen. Van Fleet, who felt the war in Korea was a "blessing in disguise," and that "there had to be a Korea either here or somewhere else in the world."[3]

A "blessing"—the annihilation and maiming of literally millions of men, women and children! A "blessing" which has brought the horrified condemnation of world opinion from a leading French Catholic intellectual like Charles Favril to the Women's International Democratic Federation!

U.S. peace forces must dissociate themselves from these "blessings," not only in the interest of common decency, but also of true patriotism and internationalism. History will not excuse the American people any more than it did the German people, if we fail effectively to dissociate ourselves from our "own" racist imperialists in their drive for world conquest and domination. This makes it necessary to deepen the understanding of all peace forces of the special white chauvinist content of the Truman bi-partisan war-policy against the colored peoples of the world.

The sharpening crisis in Wall Street's foreign policy, and particularly in the solidity of its bi-partisan coalition, is seen in the blunt "admissions" of failure from monopolists like Henry Ford II and Charles Wilson, accompanied by the attacks against "Truman's war" by a Senator Taft or a Herbert Hoover.

Reflecting the crisis amongst their masters are the lamentations of such bourgeois ideologists as Demaree Bess of the Saturday Evening Post and Walter Lippmann. More and more, these "confessions" take the form of admitting that the danger of "Russian aggression" was a

---

3   *New York Times*, Jan. 20, 1952.

maliciously conceived Big Lie. Such expressions, causing the "free enterprise" racketeers no little worry, mainly show that the peace movement at home and abroad is making it difficult for Wall Street to choose, as of today, the "all out war" alternative. It does not mean that the imperialists have lost their urge to war. In this connection, it is useful to refer to Comrade Hall's summary address at our Party's 15th National Convention: "The speeches of Hoover and Taft do reflect the crisis in Wall Street's foreign policy. They are admissions of the bankruptcy of the bi-partisan war policy. They are attempts to capitalize on the growing peace sentiments of the American people. Speeches of this kind open new doors for the peace movement. But these men belong to the war camp. We can have no illusions about Herbert Hoover, Kennedy or any one else in the war camp!⁴

It would be wrong, of course, not to pay close heed to these monopolist "admissions." Some of the forces in the emerging people's peace coalition hold that the Left does not accurately appraise these trends and that the real choice is between Hoover and Truman. Thus, I. F. Stone, starting from the correct premise that "the world can be saved by co-existence," finds Hoover to be "much closer to Henry Wallace's old position, which was also F.D.R.'s, than to Truman." "The Roosevelt-Wallace position," writes Mr. Stone "had sufficient faith in America not to be afraid of Communism. Hoover has faith enough in capitalism to feel that Communism, as he said 'will decay of its own poisons.' *Pravda* is not afraid of that challenge but the Truman-Acheson Democrats and the Dulles-Dewey Republicans are."⁵

We agree, of course, with Mr. Stone's basic premise of the possibility of peaceful co-existence. Is this, however, as Stone holds, only a question of "faith" in one or another society? No, in part the concept is influenced by "good business" reasons of trade. But this still is not the core of the matter. The core of the matter is the mass will for peace and the people's power to impose this will on the war-makers. This must be sealed in a Five Power Peace Pact. Then, and only then would it be possible to conclude that the war danger had lessened. A key to Mr. Stone's error may be found in his conclusion that "the Hoover-Taft policies might easily lead in the same direction [as Truman's] if and as new Communist victories abroad frightened the propertied classes here into support of fascism."

4   *Political Affairs*, February, 1951, p.15.
5   *N.Y. Compass*, Feb. 5, 1952.

But fear is at the heart of the present bi-partisan policy—a fear of the peoples' rule at home and abroad. History teaches that it is not the peoples' victories that lead to fascism, but their immobilization and disunity in the face of reaction's assaults. The finance capitalists move towards fascism when they become convinced that they can no longer rule in the old way; they adopt fascist methods of terror and rule rather than adhere to the most elementary democratic process at home and abroad. In resorting to this policy of external and internal aggression, they raise the hysterical cry of "aggression" against all who resist that very aggression. Thus, they howl "Soviet imperialism" and slander all movements of peoples anywhere for national liberation and national reconstruction upon democratic foundations as "internal aggression."

This policy of imperialist onslaught and fascism at home is the policy of the Truman-Dulles camp as it is of the Hoover-Taft camp. The differences between them are not of a strategic, but of a tactical, nature. Their strife is a "family quarrel" of finance-capitalist groupings, which fear and resist the peoples' victories here and abroad, and some of whom, like the Mid-Western industrialists, want at this time to concentrate upon the American and Asian continents for their "spheres of interest." They are fearful of losing all in "all out" war on the European continent.

But it is a "family quarrel" which can ripen into a crisis for the entire strategy of the bi-partisan war policy. An alert peace movement can and should enter into debate on such questions, in order to strengthen their growing advantage, to press for realization of the *real* alternative—the alternative of lasting peace, based on co-existence of the U.S.A. and the U.S.S.R., on the basis of peaceful competition, honoring of commitments, negotiation of all outstanding differences, and recognition of the basic democratic right of all peoples to choose their own form of government. It is this deeper ideological meaning, underlying the real concern of certain top monopolists with the "reckless pace" with which the bi-partisan camp moves to the twin disaster of war and depression, that a people's peace movement must grasp hold of, in order to curb the warmongers.

Main New Demagogic Arguments

The real essence of U.S. foreign policy is pro-imperialist, anti-Soviet, anti-democratic—and anti-American. This bi-partisan foreign policy seeks to destroy every "Communist State" and to annihilate every "Communist." It seeks to "overthrow internal aggression," and build "situations of strength." It poses as a "holy" crusade in order to cover its chauvinist and racist ideology as it adopts the *Mein Kampf* concept that "nationalism is the enemy of liberty."

What of the Acheson-formulated anti-Soviet "situations of strength" argument? This formula not only means continued unemployment and hastening economic crisis, but it means perpetual arming-to-the-teeth, perpetual war-mongering and forcible efforts to destroy existing governments not to the liking of U.S. imperialism. Small wonder that the "situation of strength" policy moves the high brass to express alarm that "peace may break out" in Korea, and to issue "warnings" that the flame in Korea "threatens" to end. This policy engenders, not strength, but hatred, so that the peoples of the world already compare our youth to the youth of Hitler. It is the policy of the Rommels and Mussolinis who wrote sonnets to the "beauty" of bursting shells and who gleefully watched the torture of Communists and non-Communists in concentration camps—a policy which is unfolding in the actual present building by the bi-partisans of concentration camps for "Communists first" and then for all who dare to oppose this ruinous war policy.

The more brutal "internal aggression" argument is nothing but a Truman version of the racist *Mein Kampf* aim of domination over "inferior peoples" who need the benign "blessings" of Anglo-American imperialism to lead them to "salvation. It represents a naked "white man's burden" imperialist approach of bloodily—and vainly—trying to reverse the triumphant world-wide colonial and national liberation movements highlighted by the historic victory of the People's Democratic Republic of China, and inspired by the establishment of the Union of Soviet Socialist Republics.

U.S. imperialism, faced with ever-rising and growing struggles from the oppressed Negro people within its own borders, must attempt to hide from world view its own genocidal practices, fearful lest exposure further pulverize its shibboleth of a free nation in a free world. Consequently, the fable that "nationalism is the enemy of liberty" is designed not to whittle away the concept of an arrogant boastful nation, who can "take on the world" and "get it over with quick," but in typical white supremacist manner, to heighten chauvinist nationalism and white chauvinism through the program of "imposing salvation" on "childlike" peoples to whom self-government has been ruthlessly denied in century-long suppression.

One and all, these demagogic arguments of the bi-partisans hide a policy of betrayal of the true national interests of the United States and its people. It is the Hitler dream to destroy every "Communist" state, but in the context of today it could culminate not only in world war, but in a world atomic holocaust, from which the imperialists will not and cannot emerge victorious, but in which tremendous suffering will result to our people and all the world's peace-loving peoples. What is in peril, therefore, is not the "American way of life" but the wages of workers who are asked to rob themselves of billions of dollars so that Truman and the Wall Street monopolists can roam over the earth trying to crush freedom-seeking peoples who want independence and peace and to advance socially on the basis of their choice. The peoples of the world will never yield to these Wall Street terms. The vital interests of our own country demand that a mighty peace front be built through which can emerge a people's peace coalition capable of curbing the Wall Street monopolists' drive for a third world war and fascism. Such a peace front, based on the working class and the inherently, anti-imperialist, growing Negro people's movement, will include broad sections of the farmers and millions of people in intellectual and professional pursuits.

State of Progress Towards a People's Peace Coalition

The question arises: How can we help to "build and expand" on this perspective of a people's peace coalition in the context of a day-by-day peace struggle which, in the first place, must be rooted among the workers? It must be frankly said in evaluation of the present organized peace movement in the U.S. that the growing sentiment for peace among the workers does not yet find expression in adequate peace organization of this decisive class. Necessary for this orientation and for advancing the peace movement in the U.S. by deepening its anti-fascist and anti-imperialist content, is rooting the peace movement among workers and organizing peace activities on union and shop levels. Any tendency to liquidate labor peace centers, under the guise of real difficulties, means only abandoning this perspective. There is no doubt that Right opportunist tendencies are camouflaged in the advocacy of such "Left" sectarian practices, while little enough is done to seek the precise forms of peace organization to which the workers do readily respond. The struggle to win the working class is fought, not in the realm of abstract theories of the Right or the "Left," but around specific issues, around policies as regards wages, speed up, equal rights for the Negro people, foreign affairs, inner union democracy, etc. In the words of Comrade Hall:

> We must have confidence that we can win the entire working class to the policies and programs based on class struggle. We can do this, not in isolation, but by organizing and leading in struggle the rank and file in the *existing unions*, in the departments, shops, locals and Internationals.[6]

Every index shows an increasingly anti-war feeling among the workers. More and more trade-union expressions as those emanating from figures like Carl Stellato, William R. Hood, Frank Rosenblum, etc., call for a Five-Power Peace Pact. Clearly, this higher anti-war militancy of the workers emphasizes the interlocking of the fight for peace with the fight for a decent standard of living, unshackled unionism, collective bargaining, an end to discrimination and other elementary demands. Numerous shop stewards' peace conferences and peace ballot campaigns confirm the ready response to the peace issue among the workers. Growing mass unemployment and high taxes are undoubtedly the reason for the gloomy complaints even of Social Democratic leaders like Walter Reuther.

What bothers class collaborationist labor leaders like Reuther, of course, is the growing rank-and-file pressure of the auto workers who face mass unemployment, and who are questioning the bi-partisan foreign policy which has brought them, not the promised prosperity, but worsening economic conditions. The workers see wages frozen, higher prices and taxes, and the growth of repression against the people's liberties, heightened chauvinist oppression of the Negro people, and enhanced corruption in government. Even Reuther's complaints can serve to tear the mask from the eyes of many workers, who may well wonder why Reuther and the class collaborationist labor leaders persist in trying to hold the workers within the framework of the two rotten old parties of capitalism.

In this connection it is useful to refer once again to the advice of Gus Hall:

> It was in Korea that the masses saw the greatest danger of a world war, and a war with China. The Republican very cleverly identified the Truman Administration with this central danger point, and this were able to capitalize on the peace feelings of the masses. We must conclude that, yes, large sections

---

6 *Political Affairs*, December, 1949, p. 27.

were misled. But they are for peace. They will follow the correct road in the struggle for peace if they get the right leadership. We must be able to offer the masses a practical alternative one which they see provides a real chance to win outside the two old parties. This alternative must correspond to their present level of understanding in the arena of political action [...] Large sections of the working class are beginning to draw some very important lessons from the last election campaign. The big lesson is not that the trade-union leaders took a licking. The lesson is that there must be some road that does not lead into the blind alley to which the workers have been brought by the labor officialdom. This is the outlook on which we must build, and which we must help to expand.[7]

The Present Organized Peace Centers

A basic ideological weakness underlies the tendency of failing to concentrate the peace struggles and organization among the workers and the Negro people. How is this to be observed in practice? Here is an actual example: An organized peace coalition exists in a particular city. This coalition in its present state experiences difficulty in getting a hall for a certain project. A fight is carried through unsuccessfully—and privately. Certain advanced forces in the coalition suggest that the peace issue is so urgent and the need so great that "broader forces" be sought out for this project. So far so good. Even the "private" negotiation, which should be criticized, is not the main point. Broader forces are secured and the existing peace coalition, which supports parallel peace actions, supports this one. Lo and behold! however, there are certain forces in the coalition who do not understand the Negro question, or the decisive role of the working class. Where is the emphasis of the Left forces in the coalition? They rightly express concern that this state of affairs jeopardizes the new coalition which is emerging and some of the forces in it. They themselves certainly appreciate that not all the components of the coalition will fully understand all these questions, but it is expected that they will come into the coalition on the basis of its minimum program. But its minimum program is premised on the fact that there is a great ferment for peace especially among the masses of workers and the Negro people; it is premised on the fight for labor's rights and on the effects of the war drive on the Negro people. Do the Left-progressives battle on these issues? Yes, they battle, but unfortunately ofttimes incorrectly. They usually "battle" by arguing that to struggle ideologically on these issues, would "create a problem." What they fail to recognize and ofttimes fail to do, is to examine their own weaknesses which, hav-

---

7   *Peace Can Be Won!*, p. 54.

ing their source in Right opportunism and "Left" sectarianism, usually boil down to a retreat in meeting these arguments. Experience confirms, however, that many of these broader forces respond to and learn from a struggle for the correct ideological and practical position on these questions.

Errors such as this isolate the peace coalition from decisive working class forces and the Negro people. Now, no section of a united front coalition can be ignored or "asked" to accept second class citizenship status. How much more serious this becomes when it affects the decisive core of the coalition, the labor-Negro people's alliance! Of course, where the Negro people are concerned, this reflects white chauvinism as well. Yet serious strains, affecting relations with top labor and Negro peace leaders, having a mass base on national and state levels, exist because of this most costly error in peace activity.

A key reason for such serious errors lies in the lack of a common estimate of the character and role of the present organized peace centers among labor, women, youth and in overall peace coordination. To be concrete: can it be said that full clarity exists among progressive forces, including Communists, relative to the programmatic character of the American Peace Crusade, the American Women for Peace, the National Labor Conference for Peace, the Youth Division of the Peace Crusade? No, it cannot! The American Peace Crusade and the above-mentioned independent organized peace centers, themselves coalitions, emerged as a result of the need for an organized peace center, of a special kind, shown particularly in the powerful, grass-roots response evoked by the Stockholm Peace Petition campaign. This response came from leading forces among intellectuals and professionals, as well as among the working class and the Negro people. Thus, the American Peace Crusade came into being and dedicated itself to advancing a principled program. Key elements of the A.P.C. program are the principle of peaceful co-existence and the negotiation of outstanding differences between the Big Five Powers. The program, based also on a recognition of the war drive's ravaging effects on the working class and the Negro people, spurs the struggle for Negro white unity. This peace coalition includes Left-progressive forces, and, in line with its principled advocacy of peace, programmatically rejects Red-baiting and all other divisive ideologies.

Many of the forces in the A.P.C.—and in varying degrees the other peace centers—express unclarities, and disagreement, on several phases of basic policy, including the whole question of the working class and its relation to the peace coalition, the role of the Soviet Union, etc. This is as we should expect in a genuine united front peace coalition.

But a grave persistent weakness is the lack of a working-class base and real roots among the Negro people, The point is not only that these weaknesses exist, but that many of the advanced Left-progressive forces fail to accept their special ideological role and, on numerous issues, in and out of the present organized peace coalitions, this weakness seriously jeopardizes the continued growth of the coalition. Consequently, entirely too much time is consumed in necessarily resolving these problems, on top levels, while the task of rooting and organizing a united front working class base goes by the board.

Experience teaches that where these questions have been frankly subjected to friendly discussion, the progressive forces in the coalition, together with the Left-progressives, resolve the matter satisfactorily.

All peace forces, and Left-progressives in particular, must be keen to cooperate with every progressive tendency that may manifest itself, under the strong pressure of the masses, in the trade-union leadership—on all levels—and within the Negro people's movement. All peace forces must learn to cultivate such trends and utilize them for the building of a broad peace coalition.

This is all the more decisive, since the new and increasing difficulties of the warmongers do not imply the cessation or necessarily a lessening of the war danger. On the contrary, the masses must be alerted as never before to combat the machinations of the war incendiaries.

The task demands mastery of the united front and the bold grappling with special ideological questions on all issues confronting the peace movement. Some Left-progressive forces, including some Communists, argue that the present coalition peace centers are "too Left." "We must build broader ones and scrap the old," they say. Frequently this argument hides a tendency of capitulation to so-called "broad forces" which, in fact, reject the peace coalition's minimum program. Others demonstrate in practice that to fail to build and expand present organized peace centers is to fail to take advantage of the current mass peace upsurge. Thus, the development of "broader centers" is wrongly counterposed to the strengthening of the present organized peace centers. Some Left-progressives, including some Communists, even take the initiative in dissuading groups who come into activity as a result of the stimulus of these peace centers, from coming closer to them, in day-today working relationship.

The "great debate" goes on and on, while at a standstill is the heart and core of the real issue, that of not only moving with the stream, but of building and consolidating united front peace organizations among the workers and the Negro people, and of organizing united front activity from below on the key peace issue and primarily on the economic and social consequences of the war drive.

The Right opportunist danger, reflected in a neglect to come to grips with basic ideological problems relative to the peace struggle, is mainly expressed in the failure of many Left progressives, including some Communists, to play their special ideological role of convincing people of the correctness of the previously agreed on minimum program. Nor should Left-progressives fail to note the effect that such wrong approaches have on non-Left Negro and white forces in the coalition who see their own roles being reduced and who quite correctly resent being "written off." No argument that such discussions will isolate "broader forces" holds water. The existence of an organized peace center, or even of parallel peace movements on special issues, does not excuse lack of ideological struggle in all coalition peace movements.

Conversely, the "Left" sectarian danger reflects a narrow approach to the peace movement and is based on a defeatist attitude that world war really is inevitable.

The necessity for broader forms of peace struggle complements, it does not contradict, the necessity of strengthening the present organized peace centers, particularly in terms of developing their working-class base. To pose these efforts as mutually exclusive is to endanger not only existing organized peace centers, but the whole concept of the united front, of an anti-fascist, anti-imperialist people's peace coalition based on the working class and Negro people.

Just as there is no contradiction between a mass united front coalition policy and the special responsibilities of the Left-progressives in the fight against white chauvinism, so is there no contradiction between the development of broader movements around specific peace issues and the building and strengthening of the existing organized peace centers based on the working class and the deepening of their ideological leadership.

The Negro People and the Fight for Peace and Freedom

If it is true that the Truman war crusade, brutally exemplified in the atrocious war against the colored peoples of Asia, develops in an atmosphere of rising counter-struggle for peace, it is also certainly true that even greater counter-struggle by the Negro people is developing as they resist the Wall Street bi-partisan attempt to destroy their liberation movement, and their leaders—Paul Robeson, W. E. B. Du Bois, William L. Patterson, Benjamin J. Davis, Henry Winston, James Jackson, Ben Careathers, Pettis Perry, Roosevelt Ward, Mrs. Charlotta Bass, and many, many others.

But against this white supremacist, chauvinist war drive upon the peace-loving peoples of the earth, there also develops in our epoch, the liberation movement of the peoples in colonial and dependent countries. It is clear, then, that this liberation movement "is inseparably connected with the movement for peace. Therefore any forcible attempts by the imperialists to keep these peoples in a state of dependence and colonial subjection is a threat to the cause of peace."[8]

Faced with rising anti-imperialist counter-struggle of the colonial peoples and nations and at home with the growing, and ever-more conscious anti-imperialist Negro liberation movement, American imperialism multiplies its hourly crimes against the Negro people.

At the same time there is taking place a sharpening in the whole Negro liberation movement, and a dissociation from the Truman bi-partisan war policy by increasing sections of the Negro people as expressed by more and more Negro spokesmen. Thus, many State Department Negro spokesmen are competing widely in the Negro press in "warnings" to Truman that his Point Four Program, which accompanies Wall Street's imposed "blessings," is being rejected by the independence-minded peoples of Asia, Latin America, the West Indies and Africa Thus, it is not only the forthright Dr. Mordecai Johnson, president of Howard University, who raises this issue, but even the State Department representative, Dr. Dailey, on return from a tour of the Far East and Africa, "warns" U.S. imperialism to reject this anti-national liberation path. Further, Negro spokesmen such as P. L. Prattis, editor of the *Pittsburgh Courier*, Dr. Benjamin Mays and numerous Negro journalists, commenting on recent Truman messages, warned that "Negro voters still have to be convinced." In the words of the influential Negro histori-

---

8   I. A. Seleznev, in *Political Affairs*, December, 1951.

an and publicist, J. A. Rogers: "Colored voters are convinced that they have been ruthlessly carried for a ride and exploited on the civil rights appeal. Now they are face to face with the cold facts that not a single civil rights measure has been passed in Congress. They also know that these measures have been checked on all turns by the Southern Democratic bloc. President Truman admitted in his recent State of the Union message that these issues had not been effectuated."[9]

Nothing so points up the basic new element in the relationship between the struggle for peace and the Negro liberation and people's movements than this increasingly sharp criticism by the Negro people of the Truman bi-partisan policy. The Negro people as a whole see the struggle for their rights impaled on the blade of Wall Street's greed, in a war against the colored peoples of Korea which threatens to spread into a war against the oppressed colored people of the entire world.

As decisively placed by Comrade Benjamin J. Davis in his Report to the Party's Fifteenth National Convention: "The new element in the relationship between the struggle for peace and for Negro liberation is the growing acuteness of the contradiction between American imperialism in its war program, on the one hand, and, on the other, the struggle of the Negro people and their supporters to defend their elementary liberties and to advance the cause of full citizenship. This is by far the most important single new factor to be noted in connection with the struggle for national liberation of the Negro people."

It is exactly the "new element" basically analyzed in Comrade Davis' Report that must yet be grasped by Left-progressive forces and the Party cadres. The further significance of this fundamental relationship between the struggle for peace and for freedom was documented and analyzed by Comrade Pettis Perry. These profound contributions require study and mastery by all Left-progressives and Party cadres without delay.

An appreciation of the great contributions of Comrade Davis and Perry will do much to heighten the ideological level in the struggle against white chauvinism, which still plagues the whole peace movement. We cannot speak of the new militant features of the Negro people's movement without recognizing that this very fact places new and tremendous responsibilities on our ideological and practical work. We must sharpen the understanding of the national question, particularly as this

---

9   *N. Y. Amsterdam News*, February 2, 1952.

applies to the Negro people, in order to advance the leading role of the workers in the Negro-liberation movement. This is of basic importance in the specific context of the struggle for peace in order to guarantee strengthening the alliance of the working class and Negro people. Such an alliance must form the solid core of the emerging people's peace coalition, which will reverse the present ruinous direction the imperialists are traveling.

We must put an end to the false conception that "broader forces" cannot understand the Negro question. While it would be incorrect to demand that the full program of the Negro liberation movement be part of the program of struggle of the existing organized peace movement, it is necessary to demand—and certainly to expect of Left-progressives and Communists in the peace movement—an all-out battle against the white chauvinist poison which permeates many of these movements. To assert the impossibility of spreading an understanding of the Negro question is to excuse inactivity in the fight against white chauvinism and to insult the broad masses eager for peace and democracy. We *must* convince our allies in the anti-war struggle of the correctness of the minimum program in terms of the rights of the Negro people and Negro-white unity, which they are duty bound to fight for. The struggle for peace requires a struggle against colonialism and rejection of racist warmongering. We must labor to deepen the understanding of the masses as regards the inherent relationship between the attacks on the Negro people and the attacks on the peace movement and democratic liberties, as regards the synthesis between the fight against a robber war in Asia and the imperialist attempt to thwart the Negro liberation movement and keep its leaders from exposing U.S. imperialist claims that it is a "free nation" in a "free world."

The superb people's victories in the Du Bois case, in Stuyvesant Town, and in the development of the National Negro Labor Council Movement, fused with past struggles around Trenton, Martinsville, McGee, etc., show how the struggle for Negro rights and Negro-white unity advances and heightens political consciousness on the part of participating Negro and white masses.

Merely to master the full significance of the State Department's "reason" for the denial of a passport to Paul Robeson on the grounds that "racial discrimination" is a "family matter" the public exposure of which is inimical to the interests of the security of the United States Government, is to pose the question: Why have not the peace forces fully mounted a mass campaign that can lead to victory around this prime issue involving the revered people's artist and world peace leader—Paul Robeson? All over the world, especially among the hundreds of millions of darker peoples in Asia, Africa, Latin America and the West Indies the U.S. imperialists are finding the Jim Crow system in this country a most serious obstacle in their path of aggression. And it is the Communists everywhere who, together with the Left-progressives, are the leaders of the masses in this sharp condemnation of the Jim Crow outrage in the United States.

Hence, ideological struggle on this front assumes urgent significance, particularly in view of the leadership assumed in all peace centers by outstanding Negro men and women. Their contributions cannot and should not be concentrated on "doing battle" on these issues. Their white co-workers must assume greater responsibility and initiative in this regard, not only because this is proper in the struggle for Negro rights, but also in order that these capable Negro men, women, and youth fighters may be freed to give fullest leadership, in their authoritative positions, to building a broad peace base among the Negro people; to developing relationships with the emerging peace expressions from very broad sections of the Negro and white forces, coming from churches, fraternal organizations, Negro women's organizations, etc.

This is of prime importance, since as things are today there persists a serious lack of an organized peace movement and organization in the decisive Negro communities, particularly in the South. This lack exists in the midst of rising intensity of mass actions of the Negro people against the growing lynch murders and intimidation, as in Cairo and Cicero, Illinois, Mims and Grove land, Florida, etc.

The warmakers, trying to offset this powerful anti-Jim Crow sentiment at home and abroad, have put forward a number of prominent Negro figures to belittle and deny the existence of Negro persecution in the United States. These shameful figures include Channing Tobias, Mrs. Edith Sampson, Ray Robinson and the like. These sorry apologists for white supremacy must be exposed far more vigorously than heretofore. This can best be done by the Negro people themselves, and a peace base among the Negro people on the foundation of alliance with the Negro people's movements would help greatly in exposing such misleaders. This is particularly true among Negro women, who in their significant and developing Sojourners For Truth and Justice movement, will have to deal with the burning problems of the war and its effects on the Negro children and the family, on Negro mothers and wives, among whom a fiercely powerful peace sentiment exists. All this will strengthen the growing mass independent women's peace movement in our country and its present independent peace center, American Women for Peace. Coming to grips with the consequences of the war effort opens up new and rewarding avenues of broad mass contact with the overwhelming majority of working-class Negro women, whose militant desires for freedom and peace are the most outstanding in the nation.

Five Power Peace Pact

The campaign for a Five-Power Peace Pact offers a magnificent opportunity to strengthen the whole organized peace movement in our country.

Barely five months old, the organized Pact campaign is receiving unprecedented response among masses who thus again show the error in hesitations on this question within the organized peace movement and among Left-progressive forces, including the Party. There is no doubt that influencing this vacilation was a certain amount of disorientation among the organized peace forces following the significant Chicago Peace Congress. Such moods as that of "hanging on hopes" that the military would effect cease-fire following the "ebbs and flows" of the truce talks, had to be quickly discarded, in the course of self-critical examination, for the plain truth that peace can only be won through mass struggle. Basically influencing the hesitancy was not only this factor but the underestimation of the decisive character of this Five-Power Pact effort which will not end until peace is assured by the signing of such a pact. Underlying all these factors, was a fundamental ideological weakness in comprehending the full implications of the possibility of peaceful co-existence between states of different social systems, in addition to a tendency to shy away from vigorous struggle, particularly among the working class and the Negro people, against vile anti-Soviet lies and fables about "Soviet imperialism."

The American Peace Crusade leadership in the Five-Power Peace Pact effort has been outstanding. It has stressed the many-sided approaches to this campaign and has served to stimulate trade-union, farm, Negro, women, cultural, and youth peace forces into similar activity. Numerous A.P.C. conferences on a state level and peace workshops have been held. Many petitions carrying special appeals, such as Peace Prayers, union resolutions, etc., have been issued. Scheduled for March, in Washington, is a National Delegates Assembly involving the Crusade and many other forces who do not adhere to the entire Peace Crusade program. Here delegates from the entire country will convene to exchange experiences in the signature campaign for a Five Power Peace Pact, with the purpose of stimulating the campaign.

Great initiative behind the Five Power Peace Pact effort has come from the American Women for Peace which has, in many cases, boldly canvassed existing women's organizations and urged them to participate, jointly or separately, in the campaign. Supporting the work, too, is the World Youth and Friendship Book Campaign, where signatures for a Five Power Peace Pact are gathered by young people for eventual presentation to the United Nations.

Expressions of support have come from additional varied sources, notably from trade-union leaders such as William Hood and Hugo Ernst, and from many leading intellectuals, professional and cultural figures, such as Professor Anton Carlson, Dr. W. E. B. Du Bois, Dr. Robert Morss Lovett, Paul Robeson, Dr. Alice Hamilton, and Professor Philip Morrison. Again, groups such as the Committee on Peaceful Alternatives and the American Friends Service Committee (Quakers) have reiterated their support of peaceful negotiations among the great powers. Significant leaders in the religious life of the country such as the Rev. Dr. Jemison, of the National (Negro) Baptist Alliance, Bishop Bromley Oxnam and Rabbi B. Benedict Glazer, have also spoken out for agreement amongst the great powers.

These, and many similar facts, not only confirm the growing pro-peace upsurge, but show that where the initiative is seized boldly, around particular issues, broader forces do come forward, unity is achieved, and wider and wider segments of the population are reached.

Two forthcoming international events offer further excellent opportunities for broadening and deepening the anti-war struggle. The first is the American Inter-Continental Peace Conference, scheduled for March. The prime responsibility of U.S. imperialism for the terrible exploitation of the peoples of the West Indies, and of Central and South America, makes active participation by peace lovers of the United States in this Congress all the more significant.

In April an International Conference in Defense of Children will be held in Vienna. "To save the children, the most precious wealth of all mankind," declares the International Sponsoring Committee, "we appeal to all men and women of goodwill, to all organizations which are interested in the problems of children, to participate. . . . This Conference will study what can be done in order to defend the right to life, to health and education of all children in the world." Surely, profound interest of all peace forces in the United States will be manifested towards this great international event.

The Party and the Peace Struggle

The Communist Party, whose leaders are victims of Smith Act repression, can be proud of its modest contribution to the struggle for peace. What would our nation have been, had we not had the inspiring leadership of the Party led by William Z. Foster and Eugene Dennis? The whole activity of the Party has been devoted to reversing the present ruinous path of our nation, resulting from the Wall Street bi-partisan policy. The membership, in and out of the organized peace movement, have been selfless in their work for peace, and have experienced and are experiencing many reprisals as the Communist Party fights for its legal rights as an American political party, a fight which is itself, of course, of the essence of the struggle against war. Communists must and do bring to the peace movement the selflessness, enthusiasm and confidence in victory characteristic of Marxists-Leninists, not because they are self-righteous, but because the Party is correct, because its path is the path of the development of human society.

As Communists we struggle for peace, equality, freedom and Socialism—we struggle for the best interests of the working class, the Negro people, the farming masses, the vast majority of the American people. To fulfill these high Communist principles, we must learn from the people and we must shed all moods of "spontaneity" in the peace struggle. The mastery of the united front tactic, the deepening of own ideological weapons, must be strengthened.

To work to unite all people who understand that our country is in danger of war and fascism; to work so that our nation is not viewed with fear and loathing by the people of the world; to root our peace struggle basically among the working class and Negro people—this is the path to the achievement of the correct main line of our Party in this period. That main line seeks the emergence of an anti-fascist, anti-monopoly, people's peace coalition, that will lead to a people's front against war and fascism strong enough to curb the warmongers in 1952 and thus open to all the American people a vista of happiness, security, equality and peace.

Statement Before Being Sentenced to One Year and a Day Imprisonment by Judge Edward J. Dimock after a Nine Month Trial of 13 Communist Leaders at Foley Square, New York

February 2, 1953

Claudia Jones

Your Honor, there are a few things I wish to say. For if what I say here serves even one whit to further dedicate growing millions of Americans to fight for peace and to repel the fascist drive on free speech and thought in our country, I shall consider my rising to speak worthwhile indeed.

Quite candidly Your Honor, I say these things not with any idea that what I will say will influence your sentence of me. For, even with all the power your Honor holds, how can you decide to mete out justice for the only act to which I proudly plead guilty, and one, moreover, which by your own prior rulings constitutes no crime—that of holding Communist ideas; of being a member and officer of the Communist Party of the United States?

Will you measure, for example, as worthy of one year's sentence, my passionate adherence to the idea of fighting for full unequivocal equality for my people, the Negro people which as a Communist I believe can only be achieved allied to the cause of the working class?

A year for another vital Communist belief, that the bestial Korean War is an unjust war? Or my belief that peaceful coexistence of nations can be achieved and peace won if struggled for?

Another year for my belief that only under socialism will exploitation of man by man be finally abolished and the great human and industrial resources of the nation be harnessed for the well-being of the people?

Still another year's sentence for my belief that the denial of the exercise of free speech and thought to Communists only precedes, as history confirms, the denial of the exercise of these rights to all Americans? Et cetera, Honorable Judge?

Of course your Honor might choose still another path for sentence. You will no doubt choose as the basis for sentence the concocted lies which flowed so smoothly from the well-paid tongues of stool pigeons and informers who paraded before you here and gave so-called evidence which the Court has asserted was "amply justified."

"Amply justified" your Honor? What has been amply justified? The lies of degenerate witnesses like Younglove who can only be compared to Van Der Lubbe of the Reichstag Trial? The despicable forced admission of the Negro witness Cummings who laughed at the thought of his $10,000 Judas gold jingling in his pocket when he said he would turn informer on his own mother for a mess of the prosecutor's pottage?[1]

The ill-practiced and unspeakable droning of the other Negro informer Rosser, who blurted out his well-memorized script, and even, on your Honor's prodding, would drift off into half-intelligible intonations, "I don't know what you are talking about," to name but a few examples!

"Amply justified!" Indeed! This "evidence!"

There was no official stamp powerful enough, your Honor, to dignify the obscenity of this trial of ideas. Hence, for me to accept the verdict of guilty would only mean that I considered myself less than worthy of the dignity of truth, which I cherish as a Communist and as a human being

---

1   **Ed. Note:** Thomas Aaron Younglove (died 1977) was an informant working for the FBI who joined the CPUSA on their instructions. Marinus Van Der Lubbe (13th January 1909 - 10th January 1934) was a Dutch communist building worker who was tried, convicted, and executed by the government of Nazi Germany. He was accused of causing a fire at the Reichstag building, which many historians now claim was instead a false flag attack by the Nazi government aimed at discrediting the communist party. William Garfield Cummings was a Black witness convinced to testify against Claudia Jones.

and also unsuitable to the utter contempt with which I hold such sordid performances.

That is why I find now, as throughout this trial of the ideas of Marxism-Leninism, that it is we, the defendants, who are morally free and conversely it is the prosecutors and the Court itself that stands naked before the Bill of Rights and the Constitution and the people of our country.

It is this, your Honor, that explains the not-so-strange reason that you yourself observed that we feel no guilt. For true though it is that the prosecutor has its framed-up verdict on a framed-up indictment and trial, it is not we Communist defendants who tremble at this final stage of these trial court proceedings, but the very prosecutors of our ideas.

Truly, the prosecution's victory sits shakily. For our ideas were confirmed in the course of this trial itself.

It was the world-renowned Karl Marx, founder of the Marxist-Leninist science, for which application to American and world historical conditions we were so fearfully convicted, who long ago predicted that *"The time would come when the powers that be would no longer live by the very laws they themselves have fashioned."*

In the libraries and great institutions of learning and yes, your Honor, particularly in the homes of Negro and white workers, will not such reading—which will not stop with this or any other Smith Act trial—will not men, women and youth think and ponder that such a time is here?

The thinking process, as your Honor well knows, is a process that defies jailing. When it is all boiled down, what shows is not the strength of the policies and practices of our prosecutors—which are akin to police-state practices—but their desperate fear of the people. Nothing shows this more, your Honor, than our exposure of the biased jury drawn from a system which virtually excludes Negros, Puerto Rican, and manual workers. This virtual exclusion exists not because of lack of qualifications or even financial hardship, but because of deliberate discrimination based on consciously cultivated white supremacist ruling class prejudice which sullies our boasted Western culture.

This conscious white supremacist prejudice, which Mr. Perry so well pointed out, was shown in the gingerly handling by the prosecutors and ofttimes, the Court of the Achilles heel of this alleged "force and violence" charge against us in relation to the Negro question.[2]

Introduce a title page to show Claudia Jones wrote an article during the indictment period, but you dare not read even a line of it, even to a biased jury, on which sat a lone Negro juror, there by mere accident, since he was an alternate well through most of the trial. You dare not, gentlemen of the prosecution, assert that Negro women can think and speak and write!

Moreover, you dare not read it because the article not only refutes the assertion that the ruling class will ever grant equality to 15,000,000 Negro Americans, but shows that what we are granted is unrequited force and violence not only in the unpunished barbaric crime of lynching, but in eating, in everyday existence, in living, in the armed forces, in jails, in the denial of land, in recreation—yes, even in the nation's cemeteries.

The prosecution also canceled out the overt act which accompanied the original indictment of the defendant Jones entitled "Women in the Struggle for Peace and Security." And why, your Honor? It cannot be read, your Honor—it urges American mothers, Negro women and white, to emulate the peace struggles of their anti-fascist sisters in Latin America, in the new European democracies, in the Soviet Union, in Asia and Africa to end the bestial Korean war, to stop "Operation Killer," to bring our boys home, to reject the militarist threat to embroil us in a war with China, so that their children should not suffer the fate of the Korean babies murdered by napalm bombs of B-29s, or the fate of Hiroshima.

Is all this not further proof that what we were also tried for was our opposition to racist ideas, so integral a part of the desperate drive by the men of Wall Street to war and fascism?

One thought pervaded me throughout this trial and pervades me still, and it is this: In the nine and one-half months of this trial, millions of children have been born. I speak only of those who live. Will the future of those children, including those of our defendants and even your Honor's grandchildren, be made more secure by the jailing of 13 men and women Communists whose crimes are not criminal acts but advocacy of ideas? Is this not a tyrannical violation of the American dream of "life, liberty and the pursuit of happiness"?

---

2   **Ed. Note:** One of Jones' co-defendants, Pettis Perry (1897-1965) joined the Communist Party in 1932 and was sentenced to three years in prison for violating the Smith Act.

It was in an American junior high school where I first learned of the great traditions of popular liberty of American history, for which I then received the Theodore Roosevelt Award for good citizenship.

That I have learned to interpret that history and to work to influence its change for the betterment of the people with the indispensable weapon of Marxist-Leninist ideas, that is the real crime against me.

Of all other charges I am innocent.

It was here on this soil (and not as Mr. Lane[3] would depict to the Court, as a young child of eight years of age waving revolutionary slogans), that I had early experienced experiences which are shared by millions of native-born Negroes—the bitter indignity and humiliation of second-class citizenship, the special status which makes a mockery of our Government's prated claims of a "free America" in a "free world" for 15 million Negro Americans.

It was out of my Jim Crow experiences as a young Negro woman, experiences likewise born of working-class poverty that led me in my search of why these things had to be that led me to join the Young Communist League and to choose at the age of 18 the philosophy of my life, the science of Marxism-Leninism—that philosophy that not only rejects racist ideas, but is the antithesis of them.

In this courtroom there has often flashed before me the dozens of meetings of Negro and white workers in the great auto plants at the Rouge, of New England textile workers, of students, and of women active in the peace struggle which I have addressed on behalf of my Party. Just as now, there flashes in my mind's eye those young Negro women I have seen at the Women's House of Detention, almost children, of whom, but for my early discovery of Marxism-Leninism, I might have had to say now, "There might I have been."

For what crimes? Petty crimes born of poverty, of the ghetto, of Jim Crow living, the crime of being born black on American soil, of resist-

---

3 **Ed. Note:** Myles J. Lane, the prosecutor at Claudia Jones' case, had previously been characterized by her as the "racketeer-associating prosecutor" on the trial of Benjamin Davis, another Black Communist leader. Ben Davis was one of eleven targeted communists under the Smith Act and was tried and convicted in 1948-49 (with the others being Eugene Dennis, Gus Hall, Henry Winston, John Williamson, Robert Thompson, Gil Green, John Gates, Jack Stachel, Carl Winter and Irving Potash.) In the Davis case, Myles Lane made a "crass white supremacist inference" that a Black juror could not possibly be impartial, as recounted in Claudia Jones' pamphlet *Ben Davis: Fighter for Freedom*, 1954.

ing treatment, rebellion against which un-channeled, became lawless against the very Jim Crow society that perpetuates their lawlessness.

One need only be a Negro in America to know that for the crime of being a Negro we are daily convicted by a Government which denies us elementary democratic rights, the right to vote, to hold office, to hold judgeships, to serve on juries, rights forcibly denied in the South and also in the North. And I want to concur with Mr. Perry's proposal to Mr. Lane that he recommend to the Department of Justice that they show more zeal, since they have not ever prosecuted a single anti-Semite or a Ku Kluxer in these United States with its total of 5,000 lynched Negro men, women and children since the 1860s.

I am aware that these things are not to the liking of the prosecution or even of this Court, but that cannot be helped, for one of the historical truths of all history is that the oppressed never revere their oppressors.

Now I come to a close. The probation official who interrogated me was a Negro official. Your Honor undoubtedly has his reports before you. One of the questions that he asked me was did I ever believe in any religion. I told him then that this was a personal, private matter and was guaranteed under the First Amendment of the Constitution. I wonder now, your Honor, if he somehow falsely reckoned, as many officials falsely reckon, that a change of belief or conviction in one's mature life is like putting on a new dress or a new hat? I could have quoted Scripture to him, the Scripture applied by a leading Negro religious figure in tribute and in observation of the Smith Act jailing of one of the outstanding sons of the Negro people, Ben Davis, now incarcerated in the Jim Crow Federal Penitentiary of Terre Haute, Indiana. The Scripture runs: *"Smite down the shepherd and the sheep will be scattered."*

And this, Honorable Judge, is exactly what is the purpose of all Smith Act trials, this one in particular. I share the faith of Elizabeth Gurley Flynn and Pettis Perry and all my co-defendants that America's working people, Negro and white, will surely rise, not like sheep, but with vigilance towards their liberty, to assure that peace will win, and that the decadent Smith Act, which contravenes the Bill of Rights, will be swept from the scene of history.

It was the great Frederick Douglass who had a price on his head, who said, *"Without struggle, there is no progress."* And echoing his words was the answer of the great abolitionist poet, James Russell Lowell: *"The limits of tyranny is proscribed by the measure of our resistance to it."*

If, out of this struggle, history assesses that I and my co-defendants have made some small contribution, I shall consider my role small indeed. The glorious exploits of anti-fascist heroes and heroines, honored today in all lands for their contribution to social progress, will, just like the role of our prosecutors, also be measured by the people of the United States in that coming day.

I have concluded, your Honor.

CLAUDIA JONES faced relentless persecution for her organizing and for her political activism. Arrested in 1948 and sentenced to four prison terms, she confronted threats of deportation to Trinidad. Despite, or most likely because of, her significant role in Party activities for the CPUSA, Jones was found in violation of the McCarran Act, leading to her deportation order in 1950. Undeterred, she continued her activism in the United Kingdom, where, upon arrival in London in 1955, she joined the Communist Party of Great Britain, contributing to the expansion of the British African-Caribbean community and leaving an enduring impact on the struggle for equality and justice.

SECTION 4
Conclusions

"Negro Women Can Think and Speak and Write!"
Jones' Speech to the Court Before Her Sentencing

Gerald Horne & Tionne Parris

Claudia Jones had, by 1953, been a leading Black activist within the Communist Party USA (CPUSA) for several years. Her writings had frequently drawn attention to the injustices suffered not only by African Americans, but by African American women in particular. Preceding this, Jones was arrested under the Smith Act in 1951 for delivering a speech titled "International Women's Day and the Struggle for Peace." In this instance, she had argued that women were fundamental to the advocacy of anti-imperialist, anti-fascist, and anti-racist struggles across the world. Therefore, it was no surprise that she evoked similar themes in her sentencing speech in February of 1953. It remains one of Jones's most significant contributions because in a setting which might have intimidated others, Jones expertly delivered a counter against her prosecution by foregrounding the issue of misogynoir, which was interlinked with the societal ills the Communist Party had tried to address. Poverty, miseducation, and violence were conditions intended to prevent African American progress within society, and Claudia Jones stood in front of the court and made her case as a woman who had overcome these circumstances. Most crucially, she was unapologetic about having used the "philosophy of Marxism-Leninism" to have done so. She underscored how, in a growing fascist state, she was punished for this perceived transgression. Jones' biographer, Carole Boyce Davies, once wrote that "For Claudia all writing was directed at revelation" and her speech on that day was intended to carry out that purpose.[1]

Firstly, she showed how the crime for which she was being indicted was viewed as a danger precisely because she and her comrades had laid bare the root cause of many problems in American life—capitalism. In signposting the effects of working-class poverty, Jones alluded to the growing momentum of CPUSA campaigns that had been directly focused on remedying poverty, across racial lines, in America. For example, at its core, the case of the Scottsboro Boys, which attracted Jones initially to CPUSA organizing, had been a labor issue. The young Black boys traveling for work had been falsely accused of rape by women being transported on the same train. This fate was all too common for Black men of the era and the case of Willie McGee reflected this fact too. McGee had been executed in May of 1951. Invoking the poverty from which she too had been shaped, Claudia Jones alluded that even she could have faced a similar fate had she remained a factory worker, and in these cases—the only crime was the crime of being poor and Black. She had seen as much in the jail she was kept in while she awaited trial:

> Just as now, there flashes in my mind's eye these young Negro women I have seen at the Women's House of Detention, almost children, of whom, but for my early discovery of Marxism-Leninism, I might have had to say now, "There might I have been."

In a cruel twist of fate, however, for Claudia Jones—all roads led to Rome—and she too was imprisoned, although under different circumstances. This highlighted how any deviance from the norms prescribed to African Americans by society ultimately led to incarceration, or death. The philosophy of Marxism-Leninism was, for many attracted to the CPUSA at the time, an uplifting force for those impoverished by the capitalist system. Yet, as a woman, and a Black woman specifically, her autonomy came into question. The title of her speech called out the sweeping accusation that was often levied against Black Communists and agitators throughout the 20th Century: that they had no mind of their own and instead were at the whims of foreign influences, in this case the Soviets. In the very same year, Eslanda Robeson would be asked by the House Un-American Activities Committee whether she

---

1   Carole Boyce Davies, *Left of Karl Marx: The Political Life of Black Communist Claudia Jones* (Durham and London: Duke University Press, 2007), p. 109.

had written her own book "all by herself."[2] Jones highlighted, therefore, that Black women were in fact capable of far more than they were credited for. In fact, to confront the reality that Black women, who had been dehumanized for centuries, might actually be people who were cognizant and willing to fight for their rights, was troubling to accept for some. Instead, it was easier to blame foreign manipulation for the 'sudden' struggle against the status quo. Alongside women like Louise Thompson Patterson and Audley Moore, Claudia Jones had rallied behind a myriad of progressive causes throughout the 1930s up until 1953. As a collective, these Black women had been at the forefront of a multitude of protests and had shown, time and again, that they were adept at organizing their communities towards progressive action. Moreover, these women were organizing coalitions internationally. Less than a decade prior, the American military had dropped two nuclear bombs on Japan. For Claudia Jones this exemplified the mounting cruelty towards non-white people at the hands of American aggressors. This is why Jones highlighted the importance of anti-fascist allegiances of women across the globe, all of whom saw the futures of their children and families threatened ongoing wars. She stressed how relatable these concerns were, by pointing to the fact the prosecution would not even repeat her rousing speeches for fear of convincing the audience of her legitimate perspective.

Ultimately, Jones was the canary in the coal mine—highlighting how she had been criminalized for being a radically politically engaged Black woman. In a fascist state, her existence, and the allowance of her activism, would set a dangerous precedent. Her case was mirrored by those of Paul Robeson[3] and W. E.B. Du Bois, the latter actually indicted and tried in 1951 for being the agent of an unnamed foreign power—presumably the then Soviet Union—because of his anti-nuclear and peace advocacy.[4] While Robeson was hounded for similar reasons including his passionate opposition to Jim Crow. This same contradiction would be borne out through the Black Power era as the trial of Angela Davis would echo the same repression levied against Black Communists

---

2   Barbara Ransby, Eslanda: *The Large and Unconventional Life of Mrs. Paul Robeson* (New Haven and London: Yale University Press, 2013), p. 224.

3   Gerald Horne, *Paul Robeson: The Artist as Revolutionary*, London: Pluto, 2016.

4   Gerald Horne, *Black and Red: W.E.B. Du Bois and the Afro-American Response to the Cold War, 1944-1963*, Albany: State University of New York Press, 1986.

during the 1950s. Claudia Jones, in her speech in 1953, was sounding the alarm.

The Great Anti-Imperialist Revolutionary Cause of Asian, African, and Latin American Peoples is Invincible[1]

October 8, 1968

Kim Il Sung[2]

The Treatise Published on the Occasion of the First Anniversary of the Death of Che Guevara in Battle in the Eighth Issue of *Tricontinental*, the Theoretical Organ of the Organization of Solidarity of the Peoples of Asia, Africa, and Latin America

It is nearly a year now since Comrade Ernesto Che Guevara, an indomitable revolutionary soldier and a true internationalist fighter coming

---

1 **Ed. Note:** Published in Kim Il Sung, *Selected Works* (Vol. 23) (Pyongyang: Foreign Languages Publishing House, Pyongyang, 1985), pp. 15 - 29.

2 **Ed. Note:** While Kim Il Sung's article, composed after Claudia Jones's passing and primarily commemorating the 1st anniversary of Che Guevara's death, doesn't explicitly reference Jones, its arguments continue the essence of her lifelong endeavors. The piece underscores the enduring themes of steering clear of narrow national chauvinism and advocating for international solidarity among oppressed communities worldwide—principles integral to Claudia's tireless commitment. In honoring the life of Che Guevara, another fervent internationalist and revolutionary, the article highlights the shared belief that, as Kim states, "the liberation struggle of the peoples has an international character," a sentiment exemplified by both Guevara and Jones during their lifetimes.

from the Latin American people, died a heroic death on the Bolivian battlefield. In deep grief, and with burning hatred for the enemy, the Korean people join the revolutionary people throughout the world in commemorating the first anniversary of Comrade Che Guevara's death.

Che Guevara followed the path of sacred battle to bring freedom and liberation to the people, holding aloft the banner of the anti-imperialist, anti-US struggle from early youth, and devoted his whole life to the revolutionary cause of the oppressed.

Ever since the curtain rose on the bloody history of the modern bourgeoisie—replacing the medieval exploitation camouflaged by religious and political illusions with a naked, shameless, direct and cruel one and turning the dignity of man into a mere commodity, many communists and revolutionary fighters all over the world have shed their blood and laid down their lives in the long course of the revolutionary tempest which is sweeping away everything obsolete and corrupt and reorganizing the whole structure of society in a revolutionary way, crushing the ruling circles of that former, cursed society and laying the bases of a free and happy new society. Che Guevara dedicated his precious life to this sacred struggle and thus became an honorable member of the ranks of world revolutionary martyrs.

Che Guevara was an indefatigable revolutionary in battle and a true internationalist champion completely free of narrow nationalist sentiments. His whole life was a fine example of the steadfast revolutionary fighter and true internationalist.

With other Cuban revolutionaries led by Comrade Fidel Castro, Che Guevara carried on a heroic armed struggle which contributed greatly to crushing U.S. imperialism and the dictatorial regime of its lackey Batista, and which led to the triumph of the Cuban revolution.

Fired with revolutionary enthusiasm, Che Guevara left triumphant Cuba in 1965 and moved the sphere of his operations, setting up a new outpost where innumerable difficulties and harsh trials awaited him.

Everywhere he went in Latin America, he organized and mobilized the masses in armed struggle against U.S. imperialism and its sycophants and fought bravely in the vanguard to the end of his life.

Che Guevara's revolutionary activities made a tremendous contribution to further consolidating the triumph of the Cuban revolution and stepping up the advancement of the Latin American revolution as a whole.

The Cuban revolution is the first socialist revolutionary victory in Latin America, and it is a continuation, in Latin America, of the Great October Revolution. With the triumph of the Cuban revolution, the Red banner of socialism now flies high over Latin America, which was regarded until quite recently as the hereditary estate of U.S. imperialism; thus the socialist camp has been extended to the Western Hemisphere and has grown much stronger. Today the Republic of Cuba, marching firmly at the forefront of the Latin American revolution, is the beacon of hope for the fighting people of Latin America and it casts its victorious beam along the road of struggle. The triumph of the Cuban revolution shook the U.S. imperialist colonial system to its very foundations in the Western Hemisphere and has thrown the whole of Latin America into revolutionary turbulence, dramatically arousing the people to join in the dedicated struggle for independence and freedom. Indeed, the triumph of the Cuban revolution marked the beginning of the disintegration of the system of U.S. imperialist colonial rule in Latin America; it sternly judged and sentenced to destruction that imperialism which had exploited and oppressed the people in this area for so long.

Consolidation of the triumph of the Cuban revolution is not only an important question on which the life or death, the rise or fall of the Cuban people depend. It is also a key factor in influencing the general development of the Latin American revolution.

Revolution begins with brilliant successes in one country but undergoes a lengthy period filled with pain. Countries whose proletariat seized power within the encirclement of international capitalism are threatened with the danger of imperialist aggression and the restoration of capitalism during the entire period of revolutionary transition from capitalism to socialism. The exploiting classes which have been overthrown always attempt to recover their lost positions, and foreign imperialists continue to engage in invasion and subversive political and ideological intrigue and maneuvers.

The U.S. imperialists and the reactionaries of Latin America deeply hate and fear the very existence of the Republic of Cuba and are stubbornly and maliciously scheming to crush it. They are working hard to destroy the Cuban revolution so that they may drive out the "specter" of communism haunting the Western Hemisphere and check the liberation struggle which is spreading like a prairie fire among the peoples of Latin America. While scheming to strangle Cuba by directly mobilizing their own armed forces, the U.S. imperialists are instigating the reactionary dictatorial Latin American regimes under their domination and subjugation to put political and economic pressure on Cuba and to suffocate her with their blockade policy.

To attain the ultimate victory of the revolution, the peoples who have gained power within the encirclement of international capital—while reinforcing their own internal forces in every way—should be given solid support by other forces of the world socialist revolution and broad international assistance by the working class and the oppressed peoples of all countries. In other words, successive revolutions should take place in the majority of countries of the world, in several adjacent countries at least, so as to replace imperialist encirclement with socialist encirclement. The barriers of imperialism which surround a socialist country should be torn down so that the dictatorship of the proletariat can become a worldwide system; and one country's isolation as the socialist fortress within the encirclement should be ended with the formation of strong ties of militant solidarity of the international working class and the oppressed peoples of the world. Only then can it be said that all imperialists' armed intervention will be prevented and their attempt to restore capitalism frustrated and that the ultimate victory of socialism has been secured.

Just as the forces of capital are international, so the liberation struggle of the peoples has an international character. The revolutionary movements in individual countries are national movements and, at the same time, constitute part of the world revolution. The revolutionary struggles of the peoples in all countries support and complement each other and join together in one current of world revolution. A victorious revolution should assist those countries whose revolutions have not yet triumphed, providing them with experiences and examples and should render active political, economic, and military support to the liberation struggle of the peoples of the world. The peoples in countries which have not yet won their revolutions should fight more actively to defend the successful revolutions of other countries against the imperialist policy of strangulation and hasten victory for their own revolutions. This is the law of the development of the world revolutionary movement and the fine tradition already formed in the course of the people's liberation struggle.

The Cuban revolution is an organic part of the world revolution and, in particular, constitutes the decisive link in the chain of Latin American revolution. To defend the Cuban revolution and to consolidate and follow up its victories is not only the duty of the Cuban people but also the internationalist duty of the oppressed peoples of Latin America and all the revolutionary people of the world. In the same way that the defense of the gains of the October Revolution in Russia—which made the first breach in the world capitalist system—was an important question decisive of the fate of world revolutionary development, so, too, the defense of the gains of the Cuban revolution—which made the first breach in the colonial system of U.S. imperialism in Latin America—is crucial to the fate of the Latin American revolution.

It is of great importance to the defense of the Cuban revolution that the revolutionary movement in neighboring Latin American countries should advance. If the flames of revolution flare up fiercely in many countries of Latin America where U.S. imperialism sets foot, its force will be dispersed, its energy sapped, and the attempts of the U.S. imperialists and their lackeys to strangle Cuba by concentrated force will inevitably fail. Furthermore, if the revolution triumphs in other Latin American countries, Cuba will be saved from the imperialism which hems her in on all sides, a favorable phase in the Cuban and Latin American revolutions will be opened, and the world revolution will be even further advanced.

For a revolution to take place, the subjective and objective conditions must be created. Each country's revolution should be carried out to suit its specific conditions in which the objective revolutionary situation is created. However, this by no means signifies that the revolution can develop or ripen by itself. It is always the case that the revolution can be advanced and brought to maturity only through hard struggle by revolutionaries. If, because revolution is difficult, we just wait for a favorable situation to come about and fail to play an active part, then revolutionary forces cannot be developed.

Revolutionary forces cannot rise up spontaneously without a struggle; they can be fostered and strengthened only through an arduous struggle. Without preparing for the decisive hour of the revolution, preserving revolutionary forces from enemy suppression while constantly storing them up and building them through positive struggle, it will be impossible to succeed in the revolution even when the objective situation has been created. To turn away from revolution on the pretext of avoiding sacrifice is in fact tantamount to forcing the people to accept lifelong slavery to capital and to tolerate cruel exploitation and oppression, unbearable maltreatment and humiliation, enormous suffering and victimization for ever. It can be said that the acute pain experienced at a revolutionary turning point is always much easier to endure than the chronic pain caused by the cancer of the old society. Social revolution cannot be achieved as easily as going down a royal road in broad daylight or as smoothly as a boat sailing before the wind. There may be rough and thorny problems, twists and turns, along the path of revolution, and there may be temporary setbacks and partial sacrifices. To flinch before difficulties and hesitate in the revolution for fear of sacrifice is not the attitude befitting a revolutionary.

It is the task of revolutionaries of every country to define a scientific, careful method of struggle on the basis of a correct assessment of the internal and external situation and a proper calculation of the balance of forces between friends and enemies; they must store and build up the revolutionary forces by cultivating the nucleus and awakening the masses through the trials of revolution, carrying on an active struggle, yet circumventing the snags and avoiding unnecessary sacrifices at ordinary times. And it is their task to make complete preparations to meet the great revolutionary event.

Once the revolutionary situation is created, they must seize the opportunity without hesitation and rise up in a decisive battle to shatter the reactionary regime.

The forms and methods of revolutionary struggle are also determined not by the wishes of individuals, but always by the prevailing subjective and objective situation created and the resistance of the reactionary ruling classes. Revolutionaries should be prepared for all forms of struggle; and they should effectively advance the revolutionary movement by properly combining the various forms and methods of that struggle—political, economic, violent, nonviolent, legal and illegal.

Counter-revolutionary violence is indispensable to the rule of all exploiting classes. Human history to date knows no instance of a ruling class submissively turning over its supremacy, nor any instance of a reactionary class meekly waiving its power without resorting to counter-revolutionary violence. The imperialists, in particular, cling ever more desperately to violent means of maintaining control as they approach their doom. While suppressing the peoples of their own countries, they brutally suppress all the revolutionary advances of the oppressed nations by mobilizing their military forces in order to invade and plunder other countries.

Under such conditions the liberation struggle of the oppressed peoples cannot emerge victorious without using revolutionary violence to crush foreign imperialists and overthrow the reactionary dictatorial machinery of their own exploiting classes which work hand in glove with imperialism. It is imperative to meet violence with violence and crush counter-revolutionary armed forces with revolutionary armed forces.

The revolutionary fires now raging furiously in Latin America are the natural outcome of the revolutionary situation created in this area.

The overwhelming majority of Latin American countries have come under the complete domination and bondage of U.S. imperialism.

Pro-US dictatorships have been established in many Latin American countries and their economy has been completely turned into an appendage to U.S. monopolies. The U.S. imperialists' policy of aggression and plunder in Latin America is the major impediment to social progress in this area and has plunged the people into unbearable hardship and distress. The U.S. imperialists and the pro-U.S. dictatorships in Latin America set up extensive repressive agencies, including the army and police, and suppress all forms of revolutionary advance by the people in the most brutal way.

It is obvious that unless the ragged, hungry, oppressed, and humiliated people in Latin America bravely take up arms to fight against their oppressors, they cannot attain freedom and liberation.

It is quite justifiable and admirable that under the banner of proletarian internationalism, under the banner of an anti-imperialist, anti-US struggle, Che Guevara, together with other Latin American revolutionaries, took up arms and carried out an active, heroic revolutionary struggle in various Latin American countries in the teeth of sacrifices in order to defend the Cuban revolution and hasten the day of liberation for the oppressed peoples in that area. The revolutionary people of the whole world express profound sympathy with the brave act of Che Guevara who waged a heroic armed struggle in company with other Latin American revolutionaries. The brilliant example of Che Guevara is a paragon not only for the Latin American people in their revolutionary struggle, but for the Asian and African peoples who are also fighting for liberation. It inspires them to great feats of heroism.

Che Guevara is not with us now. But the blood he shed will never be wasted. His name and the immortal revolutionary exploits he performed will go down for ever in the history of the liberation of mankind, and his noble revolutionary spirit will live for ever.

Thousands, tens of thousands, of Che Guevaras will appear on the decisive battle grounds of the revolutionary struggle in Asia, Africa, and Latin America, and the revolutionary cause which he left uncompleted will surely be won by the struggle of the Latin American revolutionaries and revolutionary peoples the world over.

Today Asia, Africa, and Latin America have become the most determined anti-imperialist front. Imperialism has met with the strong resistance of the Asian, African and Latin American peoples and has suffered the heaviest blows from them. Nevertheless, imperialism is trying desperately to recover its former footing and to regain its lost positions in those areas.

The cause of liberation of Asians, Africans and Latin Americans has not yet been realized. So long as imperialism exists anywhere in the world and oppresses and plunders them, the people cannot stop their anti-imperialist struggle for even a moment. The struggle must continue until all shades of colonialism are wiped off the face of the earth once and for all, until all the oppressed and humiliated nations establish their independent states and achieve social progress and national prosperity.

Imperialism will never relinquish its domination over colonial and dependent countries without being kicked out. It is the nature of imperialism to commit aggression and plunder. Imperialism which was not aggressive would no longer be imperialism. It will not alter its aggressive nature before it dies. That is why one must dispel all illusions about imperialism and determine to fight it to the end. Only when a principled stand is maintained against it and a staunch anti-imperialist struggle is intensified can the oppressed nations win freedom and independence; only then can the liberated peoples check imperialist aggression, consolidate national independence, and achieve prosperity for their countries and nations.

U.S. imperialism is the most barbarous and heinous imperialism of modern times; it is the ringleader of world imperialism. It is not only the Asian or the Latin American or the African countries which are having their sovereignty and territories violated by U.S. imperialism or which are being menaced by U.S. imperialist aggression. There is no place on earth to which U.S. imperialism has not stretched its tentacles of aggression, and wherever U.S. imperialism sets foot, blood is spilled.

The U.S. imperialists pursue their constant aim of bringing the whole world under their control. To realize this aim, they continue to carry out invasion and subversive activities against the socialist and newly independent countries and brutally suppress the liberation struggle of the peoples of Asia, Africa, and Latin America. This savage aggressive design of U.S. imperialism must be conclusively frustrated. It is clear that world peace cannot be safeguarded, nor can national liberation and independence or the victory of democracy and socialism be achieved without fighting against U.S. imperialism. The anti-U.S. struggle is the inescapable duty and the principal revolutionary task common to all the peoples of the world.

For the successful defeat of U.S. imperialism, it is necessary to penetrate its world strategy thoroughly. U.S. imperialism's basic strategy for world aggression at the present stage is to destroy, one by one and by force of arms, the small and divided revolutionary socialist countries and the newly independent countries while refraining from worsening its relations with the big powers and avoiding confrontation with them as far as possible. In addition, it is to intensify its ideological and political offensives in an attempt to subvert from within those countries which are ideologically weak and are reluctant to make revolution and which spread illusions about imperialism among the people and want to live with it on good terms, noisily demanding nothing less than unprincipled coexistence.

On the basis of this world strategy, the U.S. imperialists are greatly increasing their armaments and further reinforcing their military bases and aggressive military alliances so as to attack both the socialist and the progressive countries. They are extensively preparing total and nuclear war and have openly embarked on 'local war' and 'special war' in Vietnam and elsewhere.

At the same time, while desperately trying to bribe and manipulate the cowards within the working-class movement who fear revolution, the U.S. imperialists have resorted to a new form of cold war which encourages "liberalization" and "democratic development" in certain countries. They cry out for the "most favored nation" treatment and the expansion of "East-West contacts and interchanges" and seek, by this means, to infiltrate their reactionary ideology and culture, degrading the peoples ideologically, hampering economic development and thus subverting those countries from within. The imperialists are carrying out sabotage and subversion to prise the newly independent states away from the anti-imperialist front one at a time. While resorting to overt force, they use 'aid' as a bait to penetrate these countries and meddle in their internal affairs. The U.S. imperialists whip together Right-wing reactionaries and pit them against progressive forces, and seek to influence certain newly independent countries to follow the road of counter-revolution.

In other words, wielding an olive branch in one hand and arrows in the other, the U.S. imperialists are plotting to swallow up the revolutionary countries one by one through armed aggression and to subvert the ideologically weak countries through ideological and cultural aggression, combining nuclear blackmail with "peaceful penetration" and repression with appeasement and deception.

The people of the whole world should maintain the sharpest vigilance against such intrigues and stratagems by U.S. imperialism and should be fully prepared to counter the enemy's aggression in whatever forms it might appear.

In order to develop the anti-imperialist, anti-U.S. struggle vigorously, it is important to cement as firmly as possible the militant unity of all areas, countries, parties, people—to cement all the forces which oppose imperialism.

The revolutionary struggles of the Asian, African and Latin American peoples are closely linked on the basis of common desires and aspirations. When Latin America groans under the imperialist yoke, the Asian and African peoples cannot live in peace; and when U.S. imperialism collapses in the Asian and African areas, a favorable phase will also be created for the national-liberation movement of the Latin American people. The militant unity and close ties of the Asian, African and Latin American peoples will multiply the anti-imperialist, anti-U.S. revolutionary forces several times, tens of times, and become an invincible force which can successfully frustrate imperialist aggression and the united front of international reaction. Therefore, wherever U.S. imperialism is entrenched, the peoples should pool their strength and strike hard at it.

In Asia, Africa, and Latin America there are socialist and neutral, large and small countries. All these countries except the imperialists' puppet regimes and satellite states constitute anti-imperialist, anti-U.S. forces. Despite the differences of socio-political systems, political views and religious beliefs, the peoples of these countries, because they are oppressed and exploited by the imperialists and colonialists, oppose imperialism and old and new colonialism and jointly aspire towards national independence and national prosperity. The differences in socio-political systems, political views or religious beliefs cannot be an obstacle to joint action against U.S. imperialism.

All countries should form an anti-imperialist united front and take anti-U.S. joint action to crush the common enemy and attain the common goal.

It is true that there may be different categories of people amongst those who oppose imperialism. Some may actively oppose imperialism, others may hesitate in the anti-imperialist struggle, and still others may join the struggle reluctantly under pressure from their own people and the peoples of the world. But whatever their motives, it is necessary to enlist all these forces except the henchmen of imperialism in the combined anti-U.S. struggle. If more forces—however inconsistent and unsteady—are drawn into the anti-U.S. joint struggle to isolate U.S. imperialism to the greatest possible extent and unite in attacking it, that will be a positive achievement. Those who avoid the anti-imperialist struggle should be induced to join it and those who are passive should be encouraged to become active. To split the anti-U.S. united front or reject anti-U.S. joint action will only lead to the serious consequence of weakening the anti-imperialist, anti-U.S. struggle.

To defeat U.S. imperialism, all countries, both large and small, should fight against it. It is particularly important here that small countries in Asia, Africa, and Latin America relinquish flunkeyism, that is, the tendency to rely on big powers, and take an active part in the anti-U.S. struggle. It is wrong to think that U.S. imperialism cannot be beaten unless large countries fight it. It would certainly be better if large countries would join small countries to fight U.S. imperialism.

That is why small countries should endeavor to unite with large countries. But, this by no means signifies that only such a country can combat and defeat U.S. imperialism. It is clear that a small nation will not be able to make revolution if it depends on large countries and sits by doing nothing; other peoples cannot and will not make the revolution for it. Even a small country can defeat a powerful enemy once it establishes Juche, unites the masses of the people and fights valiantly, regardless of the sacrifice. This is a very simple truth of our times which has been borne out by experience. The experience of the Korean war demonstrated this truth. And the triumph of the Cuban revolution and the Vietnamese people's heroic war of resistance against U.S. imperialism and for national salvation have eloquently endorsed it.

Moreover, when many countries, however small, pool their strength to fight imperialism, the peoples will overwhelm the enemy by superior forces however strong he may be. The peoples of the countries making revolution should combine their efforts to tear the left and the right arms from U.S. imperialism, then the left and the right legs and, finally, behead it everywhere it raises its ugly head of aggression. The U.S. imperialists are bluffing now. But when the revolutionary people of the world join in dismembering them, they will totter and finally crash into oblivion. We small nations must unite and counter U.S. imperialism's strategy of swallowing us up one by one, by each one of us chopping off its head and limbs. This is the strategy small countries must employ to defeat U.S. imperialism.

For more than 20 years, the Korean people have fought against the occupation of south Korea by the U.S. imperialists and for the reunification of the country. The Korean revolution is part of the international revolutionary movement, and the revolutionary struggle of the Korean people is developing within the joint struggle of the peoples of the whole world for peace and democracy, for national independence and socialism. The Korean people are fighting to realize their cause of national liberation and, at the same time, are doing everything in their power to accelerate the advancement of the international revolutionary movement as a whole. Our people unite with all forces opposing U.S. imperialism and consistently support the peoples everywhere in their struggle against U.S. imperialism. We consider this an important factor in bringing victory to the Korean revolution.

Imperialism is a moribund force whose days are numbered, whereas the peoples' liberation struggle is a new force which aims for the progress of mankind. There may be innumerable difficulties and obstacles and twists and turns along the path of this liberation struggle.

But it is the inevitable law of historical development that imperialism is doomed and the liberation struggle of the peoples is certain of victory. The U.S.-led imperialists are desperately trying to check the surging liberation struggle of the peoples, and theirs is nothing but the deathbed tremor of those condemned to destruction.

The more frenetically the U.S. imperialists act, the more difficult their position becomes. U.S. imperialism is going downhill. Its sun is setting, never to rise again. The U.S. imperialists will undoubtedly be forced out of Asia, Africa, and Latin America by the peoples' liberation struggle. The great anti-imperialist revolutionary cause of the Asian, African, and Latin American peoples is invincible.

CONTRIBUTORS

BETSY YOON is an assistant professor at Baruch College and a member of Nodutdol for Korean Community Development. She has been to North Korea four times.

DENISE LYNN is a Professor, the Interim Chair of History, and the Director of Gender and Sexuality Studies at the University of Southern Indiana. And she is an editor of the *American Communist History* Journal.

GERALD HORNE holds the Moores Professorship of History and African American Studies at the University of Houston. His research has addressed issues of racism in a variety of relations involving labor, politics, civil rights, international relations and war.

TIONNE PARRIS is a Ph.D. student at the University of Hertfordshire, specializing in African American history, specifically the Black Power Movement of the 1960s and 1970s.

Farewell to Claudia

Nearer and nearer drew this day, dear comrade,
When I from you must sadly part,
Day after day, a dark foreboding sorrow,
Crept through my anxious heart.
No more to see you striding down the pathway,
No more to see your smiling eyes and radiant face.
No more to hear your gay and pealing laughter,
No more encircled by your love, in this sad place.
How I will miss you, words will fail to utter,
I am alone, my thoughts unshared, these weary days.
I feel bereft and empty, on this gray and dreary morning,
Facing my lonely future, hemmed in by prison ways.
Sometimes I feel you've never been in Alderson,
So full of life, so detached from here you seem.
So proud of walk, of talk, of work, of being,
Your presence here is like a fading fevered dream.
Yet as the sun shines now, through fog and darkness,
I feel a sudden joy that you are gone,
That once again you walk the streets of Harlem,
That today for you at least is Freedom's dawn.
I will be strong in our common faith, dear comrade,
I will be self-sufficient, to our ideals firm and true,
I will be strong to keep my mind and soul outside a prison,
Encouraged and inspired by ever loving memories of you.

Elizabeth Gurley Flynn (1955)

www.ingramcontent.com/pod-product-compliance
Lightning Source LLC
LaVergne TN
LVHW042157070526
838201LV00047BA/1566